BUSH SCHOOL

GETTING TO KNOW SOUTH AFRICA'S WILDLIFE

LEX HES

STRUIK TIMMINS

Acknowledgements

The author and publishers wish to thank John Varty for his conceptualisation of the *Bush School* project, Londolozi Game Reserve for providing the location, and Alison Bannister for her work on the children's activities for each chapter.

 **Nampak Limited** The publication of this book was made possible through the generous sponsorship of Nampak.

Struik Timmins Publishers (Pty) Ltd
(a member of The Struik Group (Pty) Ltd)
Struik House
80 McKenzie Street
Cape Town 8001

Reg. No.: 54/00965/07

First Published 1991

Text © Lex Hes / Londolozi Produtions 1991

Photographs © Lex Hes 1991

© Struik Timmins Publishers 1991

All rights reserved. No part of this publication may be reproduced, stored in a retrieval system or transmitted in any form or by any means, electronic, mechanical, photocopying, recording or otherwise, without the prior written permission of the copyright owners.

Editor Sean Fraser
Designer Tracey Carstens
Illustrator Janin van Niekerk
Typesetting BellSet, Cape Town
Reproduction Sparhams Cape, Cape Town
Printing and binding Kyodo Printing Co (Pte) Ltd, Singapore

ISBN 0 86978 536 2

Previous page: *Leopards climb trees to watch for prey passing below.*
Right: *Because giraffes are so tall, they can reach the top leaves.*

Contents

■	Animal Tails	4
■	The Young Ones	8
■	Animal Defences	12
■	Feeding Cycles	16
■	Natural Relationships	20
■	Owls	24
■	Flight	28
■	Keeping Cool	32
■	Spiders and Scorpions	36
■	The Termite Mound	40
■	Animals of the Night	44
■	How Animals Communicate	48
■	Big Cats	52
■	Elephants	56
■	Caring for the Earth	60
■	Index	64

Animal Tails

Most of the birds and animals in the bush have a tail of one sort or another. But their tails are not just there for decoration – most animals could not do without them.

There are long tails and short tails, fat tails and thin tails. Some tails have long hairs at the end, some have white marks at their tips and some are brightly coloured.

But what are all of these wonderful tails for?

Pouncing and playing

If you watch a lioness with her cubs, you will see that the cubs pounce on and *play* with their mother's tail. The mother lion flicks her tail away from the cubs so that it is more difficult for them to catch. Leopards do the same. This stalking and pouncing is very important for the development of the cubs as it helps them to improve their reflexes and gives them the chance to practice the real stalking and pouncing that they would have to do in order to kill when they are older.

The white circle of the waterbuck is a clear following signal for others in the herd.

Staying close to mom

It is very important that young animals, especially those which are helpless at birth, like predators and even elephants, *maintain contact* with their mothers. For this reason, an elephant calf will often curl its trunk around its mother's tail.

Talking with tails

Many animals use their tails to *communicate* with one another. Look at the tail-end of a waterbuck. There is a large white circle there. This circle stands out quite clearly so that it is easier for the waterbuck to see the other waterbuck ahead of it in the herd. In this way, when danger threatens and they have to run away, the waterbuck can stay together in a group for safety as they escape. This marking on the tail is called a *following signal*.

Follow that tail

Other animals have following signals too. The leopard has a long tail and the underside is white which stands out clearly. Then, when her cubs go hunting with her she lifts her tail over her back, making it easier for her cubs to follow her as she moves through the bush.

An elephant calf will curl its trunk around its mother's tail to maintain contact with her.

When wild dogs hunt, the bushy white tips of their tails can easily be seen by others in the pack.

Lion cubs learn the skills of stalking and catching prey by playing and pouncing on the lioness's tail.

Lions are social cats and they are even more successful when they hunt in groups. It is very important that they stay in contact with one another as they hunt through the night. Lions have tails with tufts of black hair at the tips which are used as following signals. They also signal to one another by flicking their tails over their heads or from side to side or up and down.

Another social animal that hunts in packs is the wild dog. They have tails with bushy white tips which act as perfect following signals as they chase their prey. Sometimes, in the confusion of the hunt, some wild dogs might lose contact with the rest of the pack. But they soon find their way back to the rest of the pack because those dogs that have made a kill always raise their white tails into the air – a clear signal for any lost dog.

All of these animals have permanent following signals, but there are some animals that show a following signal only when danger threatens.

Warthogs normally walk about with their tails down, but when it's time to run away from danger, they immediately raise their tails into the air and trot away. Their tails look like little aerials and are easy to see.

Kudu, nyala and bushbuck have a similar habit of curling their tails up to reveal the white underside which acts as a clear signal.

How do you feel?
You can often tell how an animal is *feeling* by watching what it does with it's tail. When you see your dog wagging his tail you know that he is happy and when he puts his tail between his legs he is unhappy.

When a white rhinoceros is agitated or angry, it curls its tail up, and the tree squirrel flicks his tail excitedly up and down in *agitation* when he spots danger, such as a leopard walking past or a snake hiding in the tree.

A lion will show that it is *angry* by swishing its tail rapidly from side to side, much like your cat at home would do. If you see a lion doing this when you approach it, then you'll know that you've gone close enough.

When a squirrel flicks its bushy tail about, it is either angry or scared.

Because cheetahs run so fast, their long tails help them to steer their bodies and keep their balance.

Rainbow colours

If you visit the Kruger National Park or the baboon cage at the zoo, you will sometimes see baboons that are red and swollen underneath their tails. These are the female baboons and they are communicating to male baboons around them that they are ready for *mating*.

Many birds use their tails to indicate that they are looking for a mate. The male paradise whydah and longtailed widow both grow long black tails in the breeding season in order to attract a mate.

So you see, there are many different ways that animals can communicate with their tails.

But there are also more *practical uses* for tails.

Keeping a balance

Animals that spend a lot of time climbing trees, such as monkeys, leopards and genets all have very long tails that help them to *balance*.

Cheetahs don't climb trees, but they do have long, slightly flattened tails that help them to both balance and steer as they chase after their prey at high speeds.

Birds use their tailfeathers to help with *stability* as well as steering and for *braking* as they land.

Safe and sound

Tails can also be used for *protection*. If a predator tackles a monitor lizard, it will immediately whip it's tail back and forth. If the predator gets in the way it will get struck a painful blow in the face and will be forced to leave the monitor alone.

Another animal that uses its tail for protection is the pangolin. His tail is covered in heavy scales, and when danger threatens he rolls up into a ball so that his tail completely covers his face.

An extra leg

The pangolin has another use for its tail – it acts as an *extra leg*. He is able to rest back on his tail to free his front feet for digging. Even when he walks, his front feet seldom touch the ground because he is supported by his hind legs and tail.

Another animal that uses its tail as an extra limb is the chameleon which will often curl its long tail around the branch to support itself.

In the bush there is a little mouse that lives in grassy areas called a climbing mouse. It also uses its tail as an extra limb by curling it around grass stalks as it climbs up to feed on the grass seeds.

Animals that live in water, such as crocodiles and otters, and fish need their tails in order to get around. They *propel* themselves through the water by flicking their tails from side to side.

Fly-swats

If you watch a herd of zebras standing in the mid-day heat, you will see that they are all swishing their tails from side to side. The reason for this is to keep the flies at bay. So that's another use for a tail – *fly-swats*. Some zebra will even stand next to each other head to tail so that they can flick flies off each other's faces.

These are just some of the many uses that tails have. So you see, tails are not there just for decoration. Most animals and birds couldn't do without them.

Zebras use their tails to swish away flies which bother them in the heat.

THINGS TO DO

Warthog tails
Warthog tails are extremely simple to make. All you have to do is pick some dry grass or bamboo leaves and glue them to one end of a bamboo stick, which should be about 30 centimetres long. And there you have your tail!

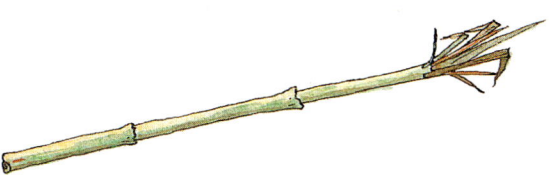

Now hold the stick between your legs and when you run lift the tufted end up over your back like an aerial. You will look just like a warthog.

Fly swat
In the hot summer months, when flies and mosquitoes bother you, why not make a fly swat – and use it just like a zebra or buffalo uses its tail to chase irritating insects away.

- Cut a branch of about 30 centimetres long and a little thicker than your thumb.
- Wind some coloured string around a paperback book about 50 times (see how this is done in the drawing above).
- Remove the string carefully and lay it flat on a table, spreading it out a little.

- Wrap the string around the stick as it is done in the drawing and tie it tightly. Now all you have to do is trim the ends of the loops and, if you want your fly swat to look really smart, you could ask someone to carve patterns onto the stick!

An elephant parade
Draw the outline of an elephant onto a sheet of stiff paper or cardboard, taking particular care with the curly trunk and tail. You could even copy the elephant drawn on this page. Make a few more elephants and then stand them in a line and make sure that their trunks touch the tails in front, so that they walk just like the elephants in the bush do!

The Young Ones

Animals have many different ways of raising and caring for their young and nature has ensured that young animals are protected from the dangers of the bush.

There are really only two ways in which animals can give birth. Either they give birth to *live young* the way mammals do, or they lay *eggs* which hatch the way birds, reptiles and insects do.

The mammals

Mammals are animals whose young are fed by their mothers by means of teats which supply milk. At first they only drink milk, but as they get older they start eating the same food as the adult.

Most mammals give birth while lying down, but the giraffe gives birth standing up and the poor creature's first journey in life is a two-metre fall!

Like many other mammals, once the young giraffe is born the mother licks it clean and will sometimes eat the afterbirth in case the smell should attract predators.

The predators

The biggest danger facing most young animals in the bush is the danger of being caught and killed by predators. Some have a better chance of surviving this danger because they can run nearly as fast as their mothers within a few minutes of being born. Wildebeest, zebra, impala and giraffe are examples of animals which are active soon after being born.

When a giraffe is born, it falls nearly two metres!

A young rhino stays close to its mother for safety.

Some mammals, like leopards, lions and hyaenas, give birth to young that are helpless. They are protected against danger by their parents and are kept in *lairs* or *dens* in safe places such as dense thickets or in holes in termite mounds where they are safe from the claws of predators.

These animals move their young to new lairs every few days to prevent the build-up of smells that might attract predators. At first the mothers move their cubs by carrying them gently by the scruff of the neck. Later the cubs are able to follow their mother.

Some mammals protect their young by carrying them around with them wherever they go until they are old enough to care for themselves. Baboons and monkeys do this.

Do you know what the difference is between a hare and a rabbit? One very important difference is that rabbits are born blind and helpless in burrows, and hares are born on top of the ground and can run around with ease only minutes after they are born.

Like all mammals, the young wildebeest drinks milk from its mother's teats.

In the shadows of the bushveld grass, zebra foals are camouflaged just as well as their parents.

Our feathered friends

There are many animals that produce young by laying eggs which later hatch.

Birds build their nests in well-concealed places and will even camouflage them by sticking lichen and cobwebs to the outside. Most birds hatch out naked and helpless. Their parents feed them and they grow very quickly so that it isn't long before they can look after themselves.

Plovers and dikkops lay their eggs on the bare ground, but the colours and patterns on the eggs camouflage them so well that they are very difficult to see. Their chicks hatch out and can run around and fend for themselves almost immediately. These chicks are called *precocious*.

Ostriches also have precocious chicks that don't even have to be fed for the first few days because there is a store of food in their necks and feet from which they live.

The little creatures

Insects develop in a different way to birds and mammals. They lay their eggs in a variety of places: in the soil, under leaves, under the bark of trees, in fruit, even in dung. The young that hatch out of the eggs look completely different to the adults and are called larvae.

Caterpillars are the larvae of moths and butterflies, and the antlions that you see living in the bottom of their little holes in the sand are the larvae of a beautiful flying insect that looks like a mayfly. These larvae go through various stages of development until they become adult.

This ostrich chick will soon be running about.

Frogs also go through different stages of development before they become adult, hatching out as little tadpoles that live almost like fish under the water.

Big families

Reptiles hatch out of their eggs looking exactly like miniature adults and immediately live the same life as their parents, feeding and fending for themselves from the start.

The Chin Spot Batis's nest is well camouflaged.

In some animals, mortality in the young is very high. This means that a lot of the babies will die before they reach maturity. To compensate for this, they give birth to many young at once.

Fish, frogs and insects lay hundreds of eggs and, because there are so many, a few are almost always certain to survive.

Big cats

Lions and cheetahs also have high mortality in their young and they give birth to as many as six young at once. Animals that have high mortality can also breed very quickly. If all the lion cubs should die, their mother would be ready to mate within a month. And it only takes three months before the new litter of cubs is born. This period, from the time the animals mate to the time the babies are born, is known as the *gestation period*.

Family time

Another way of making sure that predators do not kill too many offspring is for animals to give birth to their young over a short period of time at the same time of year. Many different species of animals, including impala, warthogs and wildebeest, do this in November and December every year and there are so many young around that predators simply cannot hunt them all.

Animals that have a low mortality rate among their young, breed very slowly and only have one offspring at a time.

Elephants give birth to one calf after a gestation period of 22 months and then only have another calf five years later. Not many young elephants are killed, because while they are small they are protected by the big elephants in the herd. When they are older, they are too big to be caught by any predators.

Who's first?

Wild dogs and lions have two very different ways of caring for their young. When their cubs are ready to eat meat, lions will take them to the kill, but they won't allow them to eat first. The little cubs have to join the other lions in the fight for food and if there is not enough to go around they go hungry. Some may even die of starvation.

But wild dogs always allow their pups to eat first. Only when the pups have fed do the adults get their fill. If the pups are too small to go on the hunt, the adults will eat the meat and then return to the den and regurgitate, or vomit up, the meat for their young pups.

You can see now that even though the bush is such a dangerous place for young animals to live, the many different ways their parents care for them ensure that they survive.

A lioness closely guards her young, defenceless cub.

THINGS TO DO

Camouflage eggs
Make your decorated easter eggs really hard to find by camouflaging your eggs and hiding them very well:
- Ask an adult to hard boil as many eggs as needed.
- Collect a few pebbles and feathers and pick some twigs, leaves, and grass from your garden or the park. Make a nest of these in a small box or basket.
- Choose coloured felt-tip pens to match the colours of the leaves and twigs you picked for your nest and carefully speckle only the top half of the cooked eggs. You could use lines, crosses, spots and small circles, but do not cover too much of the egg or your egg might look too bright and may soon be spotted.
- Lay the eggs in the nest with the speckled sides facing up – you will hardly be able to see them!
- For interest, turn the eggs over to the plain side and see how visible and vulnerable they become!

Bird nests
Make a nesting box to encourage birds to nest in your garden. Simply ask someone to help you hang an old clay plant pot under the eaves of the roof of your house. Put out a bird feeder too, and you may be able to watch a pair of birds raise their family in your very own garden!

The zoo
Keep in touch with your local zoo to find out when young animals have been born. Visit them and watch how they behave. Young baboons and monkeys are a delight to watch.

The plover chick is speckled like its egg.

Can you find the plover eggs in the sand?

Animal Defences

Animals living in the bush face all sorts of dangers from day to day. In order to survive, they have developed many different methods of defending themselves.

Before an animal can defend itself successfully, it needs to be able to spot the danger approaching. For this reason, a lot of prey animals have *very good senses*. Impala have excellent eyesight, a keen sense of smell and very good hearing. In addition, their eyes are situated on the sides of their heads so that they have a much wider field of vision. They are always alert and will usually spot the danger from a long way off.

Once the danger has been spotted, many animals in the bush will give *alarm calls*. Impala give loud snorts by blowing air through their nostrils, kudu bark loudly and squirrels chatter excitely when they spot a leopard or lion.

Animal disguises

One very good method of defence is to avoid being spotted by a predator in the first place. There are many animals that are *camouflaged* so that they look exactly like their surroundings. The bark spider sits on a tree trunk during the day and looks exactly like part of the bark. As long as he doesn't move, he is perfectly safe.

And the helpless stick insect looks so much like a dead twig that it seldom gets caught.

Impala are safest when they stay together in herds.

Marks on the Emperor moth's wings look like eyes.

Nightjars are night-time birds that sleep on the ground during the day. Their colouring is almost exactly the same as the dead leaves amongst which they often sleep.

One way to protect yourself is to *bluff* your way out of trouble. Emperor moths have large circular marks on their hind wings which look just like the eyes of a large animal or an owl, and which they can keep hidden. If danger threatens, the moth will suddenly reveal these big 'eyes' and frighten away the predator.

Some butterflies have little marks at the back of their wings that look like eyes and feelers. To kill butterflies, birds always pounce at the head, so when a bird sees these marks it thinks it is looking at the head of the butterfly and attacks. But all he catches is a little piece of wing and the butterfly is then able to fly away safely, even though his wing is slightly damaged.

Escape – hop, skip or jump?

Once the predator has been spotted, the next line of defence for most animals is to try to *escape* the danger by running, hopping or flying away, or by scurrying down into holes, retreating into water or climbing trees.

Harmful chemicals are given off by the blister beetle when it is in danger.

Chameleons can change their colours so that they are camouflaged among the leaves.

Antelope have long legs that allow them to flee danger quickly, grasshoppers and frogs have large powerful hind legs that allow them to hop great distances and birds can simply fly away if they have to.

Mongoose and jackal pups in danger will quickly disappear into the safety of old termite mound holes, hippos find safety in the water and leopards will climb trees to avoid being caught by predators such as lions.

Covering up

If an animal is unable to escape, it uses other ways to defend itself. Some animals are covered in *armour-plating*. The strange-looking pangolin is a type of anteater whose body is completely covered in a layer of heavy scales. When danger threatens he simply rolls up into a tight ball and not even a lion or leopard is able to bite through the tough scales.

Tortoises, terrapins and snails all walk around with hard *shells* attached to their bodies and if they are confronted by predators they withdraw inside where they are safe.

Causing a stink

The millipede also has a scaly body and will roll up at any sign of danger, but it also has another form of defence. If you pick one up he will give off a terrible-smelling fluid. This is called a *chemical*

To be safe from predators, a mongoose will hide in an old termite mound.

defence and it makes the millipede taste very unpleasant to any animals that might want to eat the millipede.

And you probably all know what stink-bugs smell like when they are disturbed. The smell is simply another chemical defence.

The ground beetle has an unusual chemical defence. It squirts acid into the face of any animal or bird which may try to eat it. This acid can cause blisters on your skin and could even damage your eyes. So be careful of ground beetles.

Coats of armour

Predators have teeth and claws, elephants have sharp tusks, hippos have enormous teeth and strong jaws, and antelope have horns.

The porcupine is an interesting animal whose body is completely covered in long black and white quills which usually lie flat along its back and don't look dangerous at all. But the moment danger threatens, the porcupine raises all its quills into the air and turns his back towards the danger so that the sharp ends of the quills are pointing at the predator. Then he stamps his feet and makes a loud rattling noise with special hollow quills in the tail to try and frighten the predator away. If this doesn't work the porcupine then reverses quickly towards the danger so that his quills stick into the predator's face.

Hairy caterpillars look soft and cuddly, but be careful of them as some may be quite harmful. Those hairs have stings in them that protect the caterpillars from being eaten and which cause a terrible itch if you touch one.

Big is best

The sheer size of some animals is enough to protect them. Both elephants and rhinos are so enormous that not even lions can pull them down.

Some animals make themselves look bigger than they really are in order to scare off predators. Elephant calves often do this by raising their heads high and spreading their ears.

And the black-necked spitting cobra raises its head off the ground and then spreads a hood to make itself look even more dangerous. If this bluff doesn't work, then the cobra spits venom into the eyes of the attacker.

The porcupine's sharp quills protect it from harm.

Safety in numbers

Many animals find *safety in numbers*. By gathering in large herds, impala, zebras and wildebeest improve their chances of spotting danger because there are so many alert eyes, ears and noses. That is why you will often see different kinds of animals moving together in groups. For example, the warthog, with his short legs and eyes so close to the ground, can find protection by moving with a tall animal that can see over long distances, like a giraffe.

When in danger, cobras lift their heads and spit.

The warthog's tusks scare away most of its enemies.

THINGS TO DO

Porcupine

Make your own prickly porcupine out of paper.

1. Copy the outline of the porcupine on this page onto a piece of stiff card folded in half – just as it is done in the drawing.

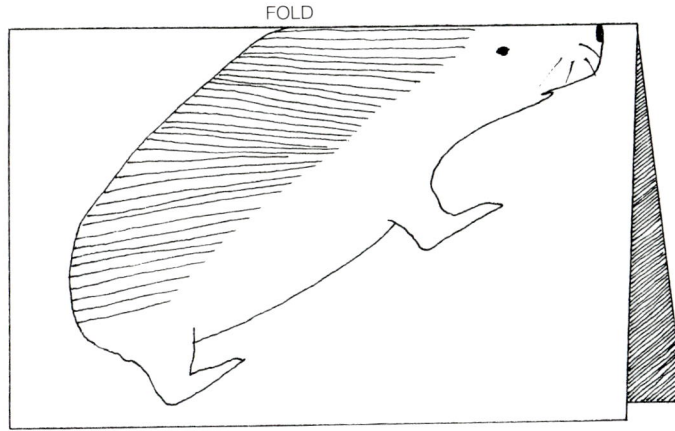

2. Cut the card, starting from the folded edge. Be careful not to cut across the fold. You should have a shape like the porcupine shown in the drawing.

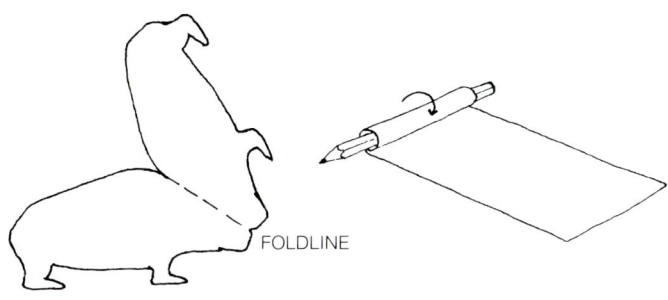

3. Now roll a piece of white paper (about 10cm x 20cm) around a pencil and stick one end down with a piece of sticky tape. Remove the pencil.
4. Cut the paper down the length of the roll – until about 5 centimetres from the end. Do this all the way around the tube.
6. Now unroll the paper, fold the porcupine body around the paper and staple it as shown in the drawings on this page.
7. Spread the legs out a little and trim the quills. Your porcupine is ready – and you could even make a whole family of different sizes.

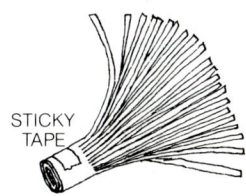 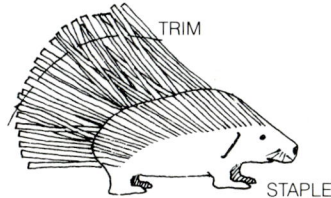

Cobra costume

1. Ask someone to sew a long piece of brown, black or cream cloth so that it looks like a long tube and fits over your whole body from your head to your toes – or even a little longer. (Material that stretches, such as tubular 'rib-trim', is ideal for your cobra costume.) Make sure that the tube tapers to a point at one end.

2. Find a water pistol and fill it with water. Then take a few elastic bands and gather one end of the tube around the nozzle of the water pistol, making sure that it is very secure.

3. Holding the water pistol in one hand, turn the bottom of the tube over your head, so that the material is now inside-out and you are inside the snake's body – just like the boy in our drawing.

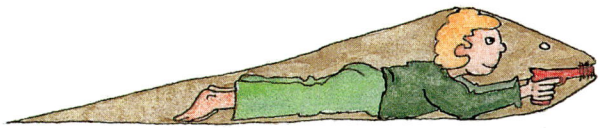

4. When someone walks past, rear up on your knees, hold up the pistol with your elbows together and held out in front of you.
5. Now, leave your hands in the same position but fling your elbows apart as far as they can go and shoot the water pistol. You will look just like a cobra spitting venom!

Feeding Cycles

As part of the living world, all plants and animals need food to survive. All living creatures form part of complicated, and sometimes delicate, feeding cycles.

In the bush there are many varieties of grasses, flowers, shrubs and trees. There are thousands of insects and spiders and hundreds of birds, mammals and reptiles. In the air and in the soil there are millions of tiny organisms called bacteria and viruses, and in the water are other living creatures including fish and frogs.

The plant eaters

The source of all life is the sun. It provides our planet with energy and it is from this energy that plants are able to make food for themselves to grow. The soil and the rain that soaks into the soil are also important for making plants grow.

Living in the soil are small creatures such as earthworms which play a very important role in keeping the soil fertilized and exposed to air.

An animal that eats plants is called a *herbivore*. Rhinos, kudu, warthogs and elephants are all examples of herbivores.

Even though there are many animals in the bush that eat plants, they don't have to compete with one another because they are able to feed at different *levels* and on different types of plants.

Zebras graze in herds and are called grazers.

Some herbivores, like buffalos, zebras and wildebeest, only eat grass. These animals are *grazers*. The grazers avoid competing with one another by feeding on grasses of different lengths. Buffalos eat long grass, zebras eat medium length grass and wildebeest prefer short grass.

Browsers and grazers

A herbivore that only eats leaves from trees is called a *browser*. Browsers avoid competing with one another by feeding at different levels on the trees. Giraffes, with their long necks, can eat leaves from the very tops of the trees, kudu feed on leaves halfway down the tree and duiker feed on leaves close to the ground.

Some animals can feed at two different levels at the same time. Impala can graze *and* browse, and warthogs eat short grass and also dig up roots.

There is one animal that can feed on all levels, from the highest branches to underground roots – the elephant. By using its size and its strength, it can push trees over so that their roots lift out of the ground. It is then able to feed on the roots as well as the leaves at the top of the tree.

Just about every part of the plant can be eaten by some or other animal. Elephants will eat the bark and roots of the tree, while birds will eat the flowers, and squirrels and birds will eat the fruit. Even the hard wood of trees is eaten by termites.

White rhinos are herbivores and feed only on grass.

These hyaenas are eating a giraffe killed by a predator such as a lion.

The meat eaters

The animals that catch and eat the plant-eating animals are called *carnivores*. Lions, leopards and cheetahs are all carnivores.

Lions can kill animals as large as a giraffe, and when they have had their fill there is often enough left over for the *scavengers* to move in and feed. Vultures and hyaenas are both scavengers, although the hyaena can sometimes kill for himself.

The different vultures avoid competing with one another by feeding on the different parts of the carcass. The large lappetfaced vulture is so strong that it can tear through the toughest of skin. The whitebacked vulture occurs in large numbers and it is able to tear through the softer skin around the belly of an animal. The hooded vulture has a small, weak beak and can only feed on the scraps of meat left behind by the other vultures.

The spotted hyaena eats any meat that is left behind and has such powerful jaws that it can even chew through the hard bones that the other predators can't eat.

If the carcass is lying near water, crocodiles may slide out of the water and feed on it too.

Food chains

While the predators and scavengers are feeding, flies are attracted to the carcass by the smell. They lay their eggs in the meat and before long, maggots hatch out and feed on the meat. And the maggots in turn are eaten by all sorts of insects, reptiles and birds.

Vultures are also scavengers and even eat hippos.

In the end these animals do a very good job of cleaning up the remains of kills.

Any animal remains that are not eaten rot back into the soil, and all of the different animals return food to the soil in the form of dung. Termites and dung beetles may then eat the dung.

The cycle is complete when plants start using the food that is returned to the soil in this way.

All these creatures form part of the food cycle – almost like links in a chain. If just one link were destroyed, the chain would be broken.

This is just a simple example of a feeding cycle. There are many other feeding cycles taking place all around us, and some of them are really very complicated.

This predator, a boomslang, is eating a chameleon.

The golden orb spider spins a web to catch insects.

The insect eaters

Living amongst the plants are thousands of insects, some of which eat the plants themselves and some which feed on other insects.

Animals that eat insects are called *insectivores*. Frogs, lizards, chameleons, spiders and many birds are insectivores.

Frogs specialize in catching insects that live on the ground, while spiders either hunt for insects on the ground or spin webs to catch them in the air.

Many birds only eat insects. Warblers search for them amongst the leaves of trees, woodpeckers probe beneath the bark, and the nightjars and swallows catch insects in the air as they fly.

These insectivores in turn are then eaten by *predators*. Snakes will catch and eat frogs, the scops owl eats spiders, and goshawks and sparrowhawks eat smaller birds.

Eating together

If you find a piece of elephant dung in the bush, you will see that feeding cycles are taking place all around you. In one piece of dung, there may be the remains of tree bark and even grasses that the elephant may have eaten as well as the pip of the torchwood tree.

Some of the pips may have been gnawed on by squirrels and other pips may even have germinated in the dung and started growing into little trees.

Underneath one piece you could find termites feeding on the dung and if you watched from a distance, you may even see some hornbills pecking at the dung to get at the termites.

There are feeding cycles like this wherever we look. In water, plants provide food for fish and insects which are eaten by birds and crocodiles and other animals. And they return food to the water in their dung.

Woodborer beetles lay their eggs in dead trees and large worms hatch out and feed on the wood. These worms are then eaten by woodpeckers who deposit their dung back into the soil so that yet another tree can grow.

You can see from these feeding cycles that the many plants and animals living in the bush are very important to each other. If we disturb or interfere with any one of these living things, we could be harming the lives of many others that are part of the same feeding cycle.

Torchwood pips may be found in elephant dung.

THINGS TO DO

Life in a tree

Although you may not be living in the bush, feeding cycles happen even in the city. Choose a tree in your garden, at school or in the local park. Carefully watch the activities of the creatures living on or around the tree and make notes of your observations.

A magnifying glass will allow you to see even more! Look at the tree sketched below. On and around the tree you will find the many creatures which visit the tree at various times of the year. Can you work out who eats whom?

Giraffe head

See how far up the tree you can browse once you have made your own giraffe head from old boxes and scraps of paper.

You will need:
- a cereal box
- stiff black paper
- bamboo stick (or long cardboard tube)
- a sheet of white paper
- a black pen
- a pencil
- a pair of scissors
- glue

How to make your giraffe:
1. Draw the ears onto a piece of card.
2. Cut out the ears and fold them in half. Glue or staple the base of each ear (the shaded areas shown on the drawing) and stick them to the side of the box.

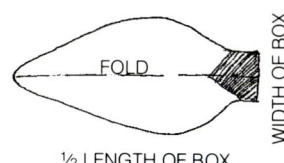

3. Cut out a pair of enormous eye lashes from black card and roll them around a pencil to curl them. Glue them onto the corner of the box.
4. Now you can paint or draw in the giraffe's face! You will need to draw nostrils on the top corners of the box and mark the mouth on the front panel.
5. Fix the box onto the bamboo stick using the back flap of the box...and your giraffe is ready to browse from even the highest branches!

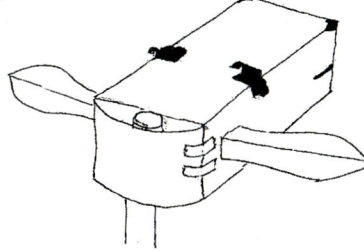

Natural Relationships

Many unusual relationships develop between different creatures who help each other to survive in the bush. Let us look at some of these interesting relationships.

In some relationships, one living thing might harm the other and in some relationships only one of the living creatures benefits while the other may not be harmed at all.

More harm than help

When two living creatures live together and one harms the other, this is called *parasitism*. The animal or plant causing the harm is called a *parasite*, and the animal being harmed is called the *host*.

Ticks are parasites which harm their hosts by sucking their blood. Many of these ticks carry diseases, and if the host gets weak from a lack of food or from stress, the disease carried by the tick can affect the host and may even cause the animal to die.

Ticks can bring deadly diseases to their host.

The mistletoe

The mistletoe is a plant parasite and its seeds are spread by birds. The seeds are left on the branches of trees where they send little roots into the tree that are able to feed on the food that the tree is producing for itself. This is harmful to the tree because it is now getting less food.

The strangler fig is another plant parasite. It carries fruit that birds enjoy. When the birds eat the fruit, the pips stick to their beaks. The birds then wipe their beaks against the branch of a tree and the pip sticks to the branch.

The pip then sends out special roots called aerial roots that can take water from the air and these roots grow longer and longer until they reach the ground. They are then able to take water from the soil and the tree grows bigger and bigger until it eventually strangles the host tree. It can take many, many years for a fig to strangle its host.

Living together happily

When two living things live together and help each other to survive, this is called *mutualism*.

A good example of mutualism in the bush is the relationship between oxpeckers and many of the plant-eating animals such as buffalo and giraffe.

The aerial roots of the strangler fig grow from pips which stick to the bark of the host tree.

The red-billed oxpecker picks harmful ticks from the coat of the buffalo.

These animals are all infested with ticks that irritate their skin and cause disease. The oxpeckers have strong red beaks that comb through the coat of the animal and pluck off the ticks. They also have strong claws and stiff tails so that they can climb up and down the animal to get at the most difficult places – under the tails, behind the ears or under the belly.

Oxpeckers have very good eyesight and, if they spot a predator approaching, they will give a trilling alarm call that warns the host.

In the breeding season, the oxpeckers pluck the hair or the fur from their hosts and then line their nests with it. So, you can see that the two different animals are helping each other. The oxpecker has food and nesting material, and the host has ticks taken off his coat and is warned of danger.

Another example of mutualism is the relationship between people and a little bird called the honeyguide.

The honeyguide

The honeyguide's favourite food is the larvae of the honeybee. But he can't get at the larvae because they are safely hidden inside the beehive which is usually in a hollow tree. So, the little honeyguide has learnt to lead people to the hive by calling excitedly and flying from tree to tree.

African people who find the hive in this way take the honey for themselves and then always make sure that they leave the larvae outside the hive for the honeyguide to eat. Both the honeyguide and the people benefit from the relationship.

If you walk through the bush, you might be able to hear the honeyguide's excited chatter.

A helping hand

In the bush there are many different examples of *commensalism*. In this relationship, only one of the two living creatures benefits without the other being harmed at all.

Starlings eat the insects disturbed by rhinos.

Drongos often swoop from trees to catch insects.

Cattle egrets eat insects disturbed by waterbuck.

The little forktailed drongo is very good at getting help from other animals. It flies along next to impala, giraffes, warthogs, rhinos and other animals, and eats the insects that are disturbed by their feet. The drongo often perches on trees nearby and swoops down on the insects, but sometimes, if there are only a few trees about, it will even perch on the animal's back.

The cattle egret and the Burchell's starling are a lot like the drongo, but they walk alongside the animals that help them.

The tree orchid is a commensal plant. It usually lives in forests where there is not much sunlight. In order to survive, tree orchids need more sunlight than that which they receive in the shade of the forest, so they spread their seeds in such a way that they land high up on branches of the trees where there is more sunlight. These seeds grow from there and are able to take water from the air by means of aerial roots. They do not harm the host trees at all.

Sharing a nest

There are many birds that have learnt to find food and nesting places with the help of people. Many birds find safe nesting places on buildings. Swifts and swallows build their nests in roofs where they are safe from predators, and flycatchers often build their nests on wall decorations or even next to doorways.

The giant eagle owl does not build its own nest but uses eagle nests that are no longer used. In the bush, the Wahlberg's eagle builds its own nest and breeds in the summer months, but when it migrates in winter, the giant eagle owl takes over the nest. The owl benefits from the eagle, but doesn't harm it in any way.

Like the eagle, the antbear helps other animals without even knowing. It digs holes in the sides of termite mounds to get at its favourite food – the termites that live there.

When the antbear leaves, other animals move in and use the holes to sleep in. Warthogs sleep in old antbear holes at night, and porcupines sleep in them during the day.

These are just some of the many relationships taking place between living creatures in the bush every day.

Tree orchid seeds need lots of sunlight to grow.

THINGS TO DO

Find the flowers
The relationship between the bee and the flower is an interesting one. The bee needs the nectar from flowers to make honey, and the flower also needs the bee to help spread its pollen so that the seeds of other flowers are fertilized.
Can you help the bees find their way to the flowers?

Owls

When the sun sets some birds of prey go to sleep while other birds wake up and come out to hunt in the darkness of the night. These birds are the owls.

Many hunting birds survive by catching and eating other animals during the day. Eagles, hawks and falcons are all hunting birds and some of them hunt in forests, some in open woodland and some in grassland areas. Some birds of prey feed on fairly large animals and others only eat insects, but all of them are called birds of prey.

The night hunters
Owls are very similar to eagles, hawks and falcons, because they have strong beaks for tearing at meat, and they have sharp powerful talons for capturing their prey. Many owls hunt in the same way as the birds of prey who hunt during the day. The marsh harrier flies slowly over the grassland searching for rats and mice, and the marsh owl does the same at night.

Owls have many adaptations that allow them to live at night.

The first thing you notice about an owl is its large eyes which are sometimes even larger than our own eyes. This is because the larger an eye, the more light it lets in.

See how big the eyes of the whitefaced owl are?

Eyes in the dark
In an animal's eye, there are two kinds of cells called rods and cones. Cones are sensitive to colour, and rods are sensitive to light. The owl's eye is made up of very few cones, but many, many rods. This means that owls can't see colour properly but, because they have so many rods, they can see in a very weak light. As a result, owls can see in the dark much better than we can.

The owl's eyes face forward all the time, so they can see in three dimensions just as we can, and they can judge the distance of the prey more accurately. The disadvantage is that they only have an angle of view of 110 degrees and so are not able to spot danger or prey from behind. And because the owl's eyes are so large, they can't move in their sockets. But fortunately for the owl, it has a very flexible neck and can turn its head more than 270 degrees in any direction. Owls can even turn their heads upside down!

Spotted eagle owls need sharp talons to catch prey.

The scops owl's ear tufts and dull colours enable it to stay hidden among the leaves during the day.

Sounds of the night
Another adaptation to living at night is the owl's excellent hearing. Scientists have found that an owl can catch a rat in almost complete darkness just by listening.

If you look at the face of the barn owl, you will see that it has a strange heart shape. This is called a facial disc, and it helps the owl with its hearing by reflecting sounds towards its ears which are on the edge of the facial disc.

Owls can hear better than other birds because they have much larger ear openings in their skulls. If you part the feathers around the ear openings you can see that each ear is a different size and shape and that one ear is often slightly higher up on the head than the other.

This is so that when an owl has its eyes fixed on prey, any sound that the prey makes will reach each ear at a slightly different time. In that way the owl can work out exactly how far away the prey is – just by listening!

To help them hear sounds behind them, owls have a large flap of skin in front of the ear which they can raise and lower. If you cup your hand in front of your ear so that the cupped hand is facing backwards, you will find that it is possible to hear sounds behind your head more clearly. The owl's ear-flaps work in much the same way.

Flying in silence
Did you know that owls' wings are adapted to help them with their hearing? Most birds' wings are made up of stiff feathers that make a noise when the wing flaps, but the owl's flight feathers have soft edges that reduce the noisy sound of air rushing over the wings. Because they fly silently, owls are able to hear the rustle of rats in the grass, even as they fly.

Another advantage of flying silently, is that rats and mice are not able to hear the owl approaching.

What about the ear tufts we see on the heads of many owls? They are not really ears at all, but just feathers the owl uses to camouflage itself.

The spotted eagle owl's feathers serve as camouflage.

The heart-shaped face of the barn owl enables it to hear very well.

Owl disguises

Most owls have what is called 'cryptic coloration'. This means that they are coloured in such a way that they look like their surroundings. Many owls look just like the bark of a tree. During the day, when they go to sleep, owls find a suitable tree and then settle down next to the trunk so that their colouring blends in perfectly with the tree bark. They then raise their ear tufts so that they look a bit like a jagged tree stump.

Hoots, grunts and whistles

You probably know what an owl sounds like. Many of you would have read about owls going '*too whit too-woo*', but owls make many different sounds. Some owls hoot loudly, some grunt, others trill and whistle, while some may even make strange ghostly sounds.

The reasons that owls call so much is because they are territorial. This means that each pair of owls has an area which it defends, and they tell other owls that the area is occupied by calling.

Who's the boss?

But owls of different types can live together in the same territory. This is because each type of owl feeds on different food and hunts in different ways. The scops owl and the barred owl live together in similar habitats, but they feed on different foods; the scops owl on spiders and insects, and the barred owl on rats and mice.

Owls can be very helpful to people because they catch and kill animals that are pests. One barn owl must eat at least three rats every night to survive. If that barn owl has one mate and five chicks, he would be killing 21 rats every night. So, you can see how useful an owl can be.

But many owls are being killed accidentally because people try to poison rats and insects. Owls will eat these poisoned animals and the more animals they eat, the more poison they swallow until eventually they die. We must try to remember that the owls could be controlling these pests themselves.

Spotted eagle owl chicks are raised in hollow tree trunks.

THINGS TO DO

Your own balloon owl
Make your own spotted balloon owl out of papier-mâché.
- Blow up a round balloon until it is quite hard and knot the opening.
- Tear a few pages of newspaper into squares so that each side measures 5 centimetres.
- Soak the newspaper squares in glue, remove the excess glue and cover the balloon with overlapping pieces of paper. Allow the first layer to dry before you add the other layers.
- Lay at least four layers, making sure the balloon is equally covered all around. Allow the last layer to dry before you continue with the next step.
- Cut a small slit into the newspaper shell and burst the balloon.
- Paint over the newspaper with poster paint.
- Cut out a pair of talons from stiff card as shown in the drawing and glue the talons to the balloon shell.

- Draw a pair of large round eyes directly onto the shell or cut out a pair and glue them to the shell. Don't forget to also make a beak for your owl.
- Draw some feathers onto a piece of paper and carefully cut them out – or collect real feathers from the local park or zoo. Glue them onto the sides of the owl for wings (start at the feet and work upwards, overlapping them so that the feathers look even more realistic!).

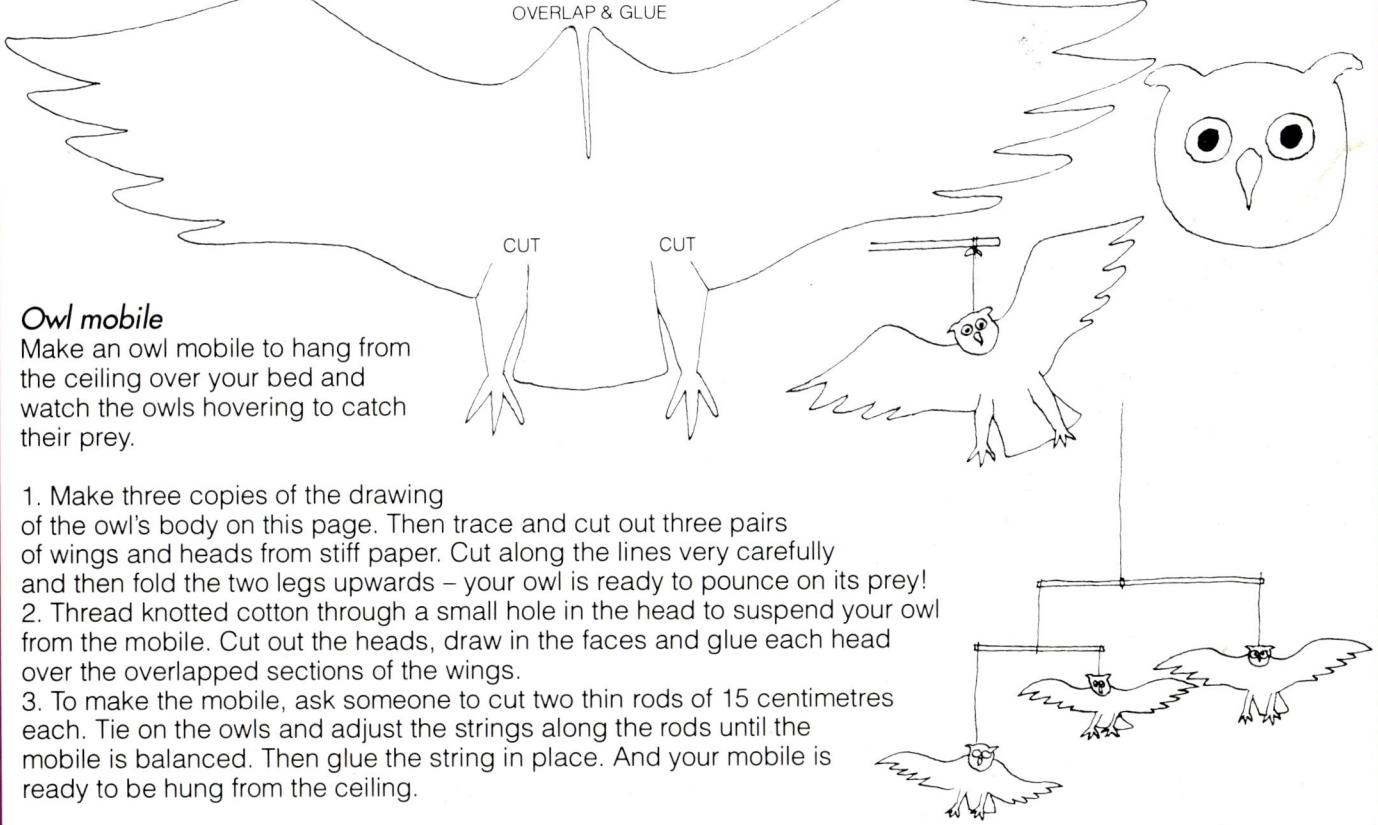

Owl mobile
Make an owl mobile to hang from the ceiling over your bed and watch the owls hovering to catch their prey.

1. Make three copies of the drawing of the owl's body on this page. Then trace and cut out three pairs of wings and heads from stiff paper. Cut along the lines very carefully and then fold the two legs upwards – your owl is ready to pounce on its prey!
2. Thread knotted cotton through a small hole in the head to suspend your owl from the mobile. Cut out the heads, draw in the faces and glue each head over the overlapped sections of the wings.
3. To make the mobile, ask someone to cut two thin rods of 15 centimetres each. Tie on the owls and adjust the strings along the rods until the mobile is balanced. Then glue the string in place. And your mobile is ready to be hung from the ceiling.

Flight

Many birds have beautiful colours, make a variety of sounds and can be found just about anywhere in the world, but the most amazing fact about birds is that they fly.

Birds can fly quickly and slowly, high up in the air or close to the ground; they can fly in large flocks twisting and turning or they can fly alone, darting through the trees of a forest or above the surface of the sea. They can soar, dive, hover and glide. Some birds can even fly backwards! How do they do it?

Built to fly

The reason why birds fly so well is that they are designed to fly. In order to fly, an animal needs lots of power to get off the ground and it also has to be streamlined and light in weight.

A bird's skeleton is extremely light. This is because most of the bones in a bird's body are hollow, unlike our bones which are large, solid and very heavy. Even though they are hollow, birds' bones are strong too, because they are supported by little bars that fit across the hollows.

Smooth feathers help streamline birds in flight.

To make them lighter so that they can fly, the bones of most birds are almost hollow.

As time flies by

Over the years, birds have also lost unnecessary features which might add to their weight. They do not have a heavy jawbone with large heavy teeth like we do. Instead, they have a small light beak.

Most mammals and reptiles have long tails made up of many bones, but birds have lost these tail bones and in their place is a single flat bone to which the tail feathers are attached.

And many of the finger bones found in mammals do not exist in the bird's wings. These features make the skeleton so much lighter.

To help them fly, birds have extremely efficient circulation and breathing systems. Their lungs are very large and are even connected to the hollows in the bones and to airsacs in the muscles so that every time a bird breathes in, its bones and the muscles fill up with air, giving it more oxygen and making the bird even lighter.

The heart is also much larger than the hearts of other animals of a similar size. This means that more blood can be pumped through the body of the bird to help with the circulation of oxygen.

Because its feathers overlap, air flows easily over the bird's streamlined body when it flies.

Its strong tail feathers and the air flowing over its wings help to carry the kelp gull as it flies.

Instead of being covered in a heavy furry skin like most mammals, birds are clothed in layers of feathers which are very light and strong. It is these feathers that streamline the bird. They lie across the bird's body and allow the air to flow evenly over the bird.

Birds have no external ears protruding from their heads that would interfere with the flow of air. Instead, the bird's ears are well hidden under the feathers on the side of the head. And when the bird takes off, it folds its legs comfortably under its tail to keep them out of the way.

The power of wings

To become airborne, birds need power to flap their wings. Most of a bird's muscles are not well-developed except for the most important muscles of all, the chest muscles. It is these muscles that give the bird the strength to flap its wings up and down.

Just as a car needs petrol to drive its engine, so a bird needs energy to fly. Most of the smaller birds eat low-calorie, high-energy food such as insects, pollen, seeds and fruit while many of the larger birds get their energy from eating fish; other birds, reptiles and mammals.

Birds take off into the air in a number of different ways. Most birds just jump upwards to give their wings enough room to flap and then fly away. But some birds don't have legs that are strong enough to jump, and they have to leap from their perches in trees or from cliffs into the air with their wings outstretched.

Some birds need a runway to take off. They run with their wings spread out until their speed takes them into the air. Some birds, like albatrosses, need a strong wind to become airborne. If there is no wind, they do not fly.

Is it a bird or is it a plane?

If you look at a cross-section of a wing you will see that it is shaped much like an aeroplane's wings – convex above and concave below. Because of this shape, the air flowing over the top of the wing moves faster than the air below and this results in a difference in pressure which causes the wing to rise, carrying the bird with it.

Albatrosses need strong winds to help them lift their heavy bodies into the air.

The saddlebill stork has long flight feathers.

Strong chest muscles help birds to flap their wings.

As the bird flaps its wings, its primary feathers twist backwards and forwards and this feather movement pushes the bird forwards in the same way that a propeller pushes an aeroplane forward.

As the bird flaps its wings downwards, the feathers are flattened together and push the air backwards. As the wing flaps upwards, the feathers twist and separate and allow air to pass between them before closing again for the next downwards flap.

Once in the air, the bird uses a combination of wing and tail movements to stay in control. To dive downwards and to increase speed, the wings are swept back and folded slightly. To rise upwards, the wings are swept forward and straightened.

By raising or lowering either wing, the bird is able to turn. The tail helps the bird to turn by twisting one way or the other.

Birds can increase their stability in the air by allowing their wings to form a shallow V.

Using the wind and air

Larger birds with broad wings – like storks, vultures and eagles – save energy by soaring. They make use of rising columns of warm air called thermals. These thermals lift the bird higher and higher into the air. When it is high enough, the bird glides slowly down in the direction it wants to go until it reaches another thermal.

Birds are very clever at making use of other updraughts of air that occur on cliff faces, over ocean swells and in areas of bad weather.

The albatross uses the wind very cleverly to fly just above the surface of the sea. It flies into the wind to gain lift and, when it is high enough it turns away from the wind to gain speed. Near the surface of the sea there is a cushion of air that keeps it airborne and if it wants height, the bird turns into the wind again.

The feet and tail feathers of the Cape gannet act as brakes when the bird comes in to land.

Why do birds fly?

What are the advantages of flying? Flying allows birds of prey, such as eagles and hawks, to sneak up on their prey, it allows birds to escape danger and to travel great distances if necessary in search of food.

When it is time for a bird to land, it swivels its wings backwards so that it begins to stall. At the same time, it flaps its wings quickly to stop itself from falling out of the sky, and its feet and tail act as brakes.

So you can see from all of this, that we will probably never be able to fly like a bird. We are just not designed for flying.

THINGS TO DO

Fun with flying
By making your own paper aeroplane, you can see how birds use the air and the wind to fly.

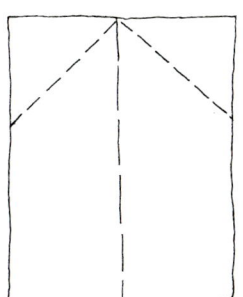 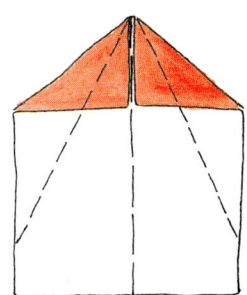

1. Take an A4 sheet of paper and fold it in half along its length. Then open it out and lie it flat. Fold in the two corners towards the centre of the page as shown by the dotted lines in the drawing.
2. Once again, fold the two sides along the dotted lines shown.

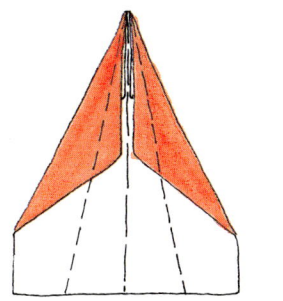 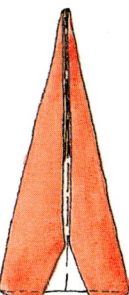

3. Then fold the paper once more towards the centre.
4. Make a crease in the wing tips along the dotted lines and leave them flat. Then fold the model in half – backwards along the dotted line.

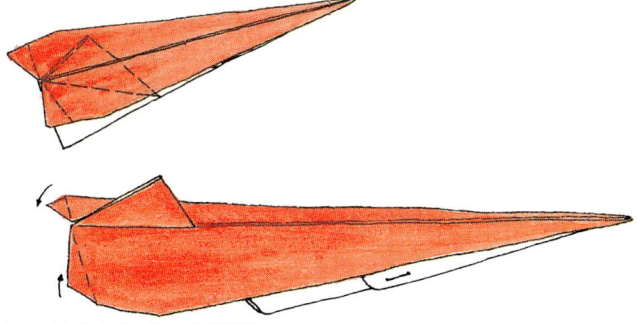

ADJUST FLAPS UP OR DOWN

5. Staple the underside of the body together.
6. Finally, fold the wing tips up for 'looping the loop' and down for diving. What will your plane do when one wing tip is turned down and one is turned up?

Now that you have made an aeroplane, you could make a helicopter too!

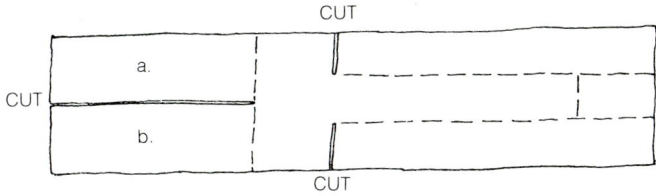

1. Take a sheet of paper (30 cm x 7 cm) and make cuts in the three places shown in the drawing.
2. Fold the two flaps on the left side, (a) and (b), along the dotted lines – one forward and one backward. Fold the edges on the right side along the dotted lines, and then turn up the end and staple it down. Your paper helicopter should fly beautifully, spiralling from as high as possible!

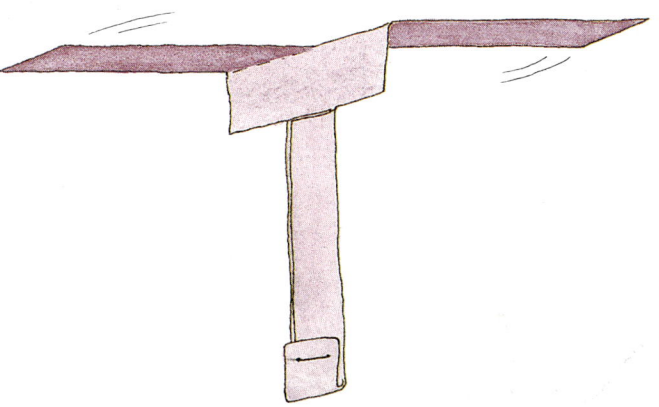

A flock of gulls in flight.

Keeping Cool

Just as we all have different ways of keeping cool, so the different animals have methods of keeping their body temperature down in the heat of the bush.

What do you do to cool yourself on a hot summer day? Jump into a cool swimming pool? Drink an ice-cold glass of water? Or what about eating an ice-cream?

Most animals in the bush have fur or feathers over their bodies that help to protect them against the heat and the cold. But what about the animals that don't, like rhinos, warthogs and buffalo?

Taking a mud bath

In summer, when it is very hot and the rains have filled all the waterholes, these animals will lie in the cool water, sometimes for hours at a time.

Sometimes there is mud in the waterholes and the bare-skinned animals will wallow in the mud until their bodies are completely covered. When they leave the waterhole the mud dries and protects them from the sun.

Because hippos have sensitive skin, they stay in the water during most of the day.

Hippos have completely bare skins that are so sensitive to the sun's rays that they would die of sunstroke if they didn't have a way of keeping cool. They solve this problem by sleeping in the cool water of the river throughout the day and only come out of the water to graze at night.

Elephants also have bare skins, and they keep cool by spraying water over themselves with their trunks which can hold more than 20 litres at a time. They also roll and wallow in the mud like warthogs and rhinos.

Built-in fans

But elephants have another interesting way of keeping cool. Their enormous ears have a network of fine blood vessels in them. All the blood in the elephant's body flows through these vessels and, when it is hot, the elephant flaps its ears back and forth. This causes the blood in the ears to cool down and it then returns to the body at a lower temperature. The elephant's ears work exactly like the radiator of a car.

Elephants flap their big ears to keep cool.

The gemsbok has a special cooling system in its nose which helps keep it cool.

The giraffe, like most animals in the bush, keeps its temperature down by drinking from waterholes.

Another animal that has a 'built-in fan' is the gemsbok. It lives in the Kalahari Desert where it is very hot, so it is important to keep cool. Its radiator system is in its nose. All the blood in the body of the gemsbok flows through a network of blood vessels in the nose, and as it breathes in and out, the air passing through the nostrils cools the blood.

After you have played with your dog on a hot day you will see it pant. Lions and leopards also pant when they are hot. There is a fine network of small blood vessels on the tongue and the panting draws air across the tongue which cools the blood in the vessels.

Crocodiles open their mouths when they are hot and they are kept cool in a similar way.

Birds also keep cool by panting.

One way to keep cool is to drink water from the many waterholes in the bush and another way is to stand in the shade of a tree.

Shelter in the shade

In hot parts of the world such as the bushveld of southern Africa, most of the animals spend the hottest part of the day resting and are only active when the weather becomes cool. Antelope such as kudu, impala and waterbuck all rest in the shade during the heat of the day. Lions spend the whole day sleeping and only wake up to hunt once it gets dark. And there are many, many other animals that avoid the blazing sun by only moving around at night.

Crocodiles hold their mouths open so that air can cool the blood passing through their tongues.

The cold and wet mud helps the buffalo to keep its temperature down.

Some animals are clever enough to build temperature controls into their homes. Termites live in large termite mounds which often stand in the blazing sun, but they are able to keep the inside of the mound cool by means of ventilation shafts which they can open and close as the temperature outside the mound changes.

If it is too hot even for the ventilation shafts, then the termites also have another very clever way of keeping the mound cool. They have tunnels that go deep down into the earth to underground water and they use these tunnels to collect water which they carry up to the top of the mound. The wind blows across the wet earth and cools the mound.

Tree houses

Another animal that builds a home that is cool, is the sociable weaver. These little birds live in flocks in the Kalahari Desert where it gets very hot, especially in summer when the birds breed. They build enormous nests made of grass that are sometimes as big as double decker buses. The grass is piled up very high and underneath the structure are little openings where the birds actually nest. The pile of grass above the nests acts as perfect protection against the heat of the Kalahari Desert.

Birds also keep cool by flying. The air flowing over the bird's body keeps it cool and, by gliding as often as possible, the bird is able to save energy which would otherwise produce heat.

These are just some of the many different ways that animals in the bush are able to keep cool.

Lions drink from waterholes to stay cool.

Warthogs also enjoy wallowing in the cool mud.

THINGS TO DO

Keeping cool
Which of these animals wallow in muddy water to keep cool?

Many animals use parts of their own body to keep cool on hot days. Can you match the animal with their own 'cooling systems'?

1. elephant   a. nose
2. gemsbok   b. wings
3. dog   c. ears
4. birds   d. tongue

1. _____
2. _____
3. _____
4. _____

Answers: hippo, buffalo, warthog, elephant, crocodile.

Answers: 1 – c; 2 – a; 3 – d; 4 – b

Spiders and Scorpions

Arachnids are odd creatures with eight legs and some may look very scary. There are lots of different types, but the ones we know best are the spiders and scorpions.

What would you do if you saw a scorpion creeping along the floor of your bedroom, or a spider sitting on the wall? Most people would scream for help or even kill these small creepy crawly creatures. But if you and I knew more about them, we would find that they are really not so scary after all.

A sting in the tail

Arachnids all have eight legs and include whip-scorpions, ticks and mites, but scorpions are probably the scariest.

Scorpions are mean-looking creatures with pincers in the front and a long tail with a sting at the back. They use their pincers to catch their insect prey and their sting to inject poison into their prey.

There are 175 different species of scorpions in South Africa and all of them are active at night. Some scorpions dig burrows which they live in; others live under rocks or under the bark of trees and still others live in cracks in rocks. At night they sit at the entrances of their homes and wait for insects to come past which they then catch with their pincers.

The creeping scorpion has a pair of strong pincers to catch its prey.

Scorpions are camouflaged against the bark of trees.

Scorpions come in a variety of different sizes. Some are as small as your little fingernail and others can be nearly as long as a ruler.

There are two types of scorpions: ones with thick tails and small pincers, and ones with thin tails and large pincers. Both kinds look very mean but the thick-tailed scorpions are the most dangerous.

The black, hairy, thick-tailed scorpion is very large and has a large, thick, hairy tail which it carries above its head as it moves about. It lives under rocks in dry areas and comes out at night to hunt for insects.

Putting up a fight

If you were to disturb this scorpion by touching it with a stick, two things would happen. First it would make a loud rattling noise to frighten you away. If you look closely, you will see that the scorpion is making the noise by scratching the end of its tail against the hard shell at the base of its long tail.

Scorpion stings inject poison which paralyses prey.

A web is made of thin threads spun by the spider.

Then, if that doesn't frighten you, the scorpion is able to squirt venom at you from the sting at the end of its tail. If this venom gets into your eyes it can cause terrible pain.

So be careful of scorpions that have thick tails and small pincers. They can be very dangerous.

There is one scorpion that is so gentle that it is possible to pick it up if you handle it very carefully. It is called the rock scorpion and it has a flattened body so that it can live in small cracks amongst rocks. Some rock scorpions can be very big, but they have long thin tails which tells us that they are not so dangerous.

The yellow-legged creeping scorpion is another thin-tailed scorpion that lives in burrows under the ground. These burrows are easy to find because they have an opening that is long and narrow. The scorpion sleeps in the burrow all day and then comes out at night to hunt for insects.

The web spinners

Did you know that there are over 4 000 different species of spiders in South Africa? Spiders can be found just about everywhere – in trees, on the ground, in houses, under rocks, in the sand, and even in water.

Although many spiders look big and hairy and nasty, very few are dangerous.

Many spiders spin webs with a sticky silk thread which they use to capture flying insects.

The golden orb-web spider spins a large circular web called an orb between two trees. It is a beautiful yellow and black spider that can grow larger than your hand and it sits in the middle of the web and waits for insects to fly into it. The silk from which the web is made is very strong, so the spider is able to catch large insects. Sometimes birds may even be caught.

The web's sticky threads trap the spider's prey.

A silky trap

When an insect lands in the web, the spider runs up to it and immediately spins silk around it to trap it more firmly. Then the spider injects venom into the insect by biting it. After a few minutes, the insect dies and the spider is able to eat it.

The bark spider also spins a large orb web, but it only does so at night. It sits in the centre of the web all night long, catching insects that fly into it. In the morning it does a strange thing. It actually dismantles the web, rolls it up into a ball and then eats it. Then it sits on the branch of a tree where its colouring looks exactly the same as the tree bark. The bark spider stays there for the day and at night it spins a new web.

Spiders spin many types of interesting webs, but the most common is the orb web.

The button that can kill

There are many other spiders that spin webs, but there is only one that you have to be really careful of - the black button spider.

It is a small black spider with a round body and a red mark on its back. Although it is the most poisonous spider in South Africa, it is very shy and will only bite if you accidentally squash it. It is usually found among rocks in long grass where it spins a small untidy web.

Another interesting web-spinner is the social spider. These spiders are very unusual because they live together in large groups. They spin a large untidy nest on the ends of tree branches and they live in the centre of the nest. Insects are then entangled in strands of silk that radiate from the centre of the nest and the spiders all rush out and attack the insect.

Spiders on the ground

There are many spiders that do not spin webs.

Hunting spiders such as the wolf spider live in small holes in the ground and come out and hunt insects at night by running them down.

Baboon spiders are big hairy spiders that live in large silk-lined burrows in the ground. They hunt their insect prey by waiting for insects to come past their burrows at night and then quickly rush forward to catch them. They probably get their names because they are hairy like baboons.

There are many, many other spiders all around us: jumping spiders, wandering spiders, spitting spiders and bolas spiders. There is even a spider that catches fish.

All of them are fascinating, and both spiders and scorpions are very useful because they play an important role in controlling insect populations.

So think carefully before you kill that scary, hairy, creepy-crawly spider sitting on the wall.

The golden orb spider on its characteristic web.

Hunting spiders live in small holes in the ground.

THINGS TO DO

Spider webs

Get up early one morning and go on a spider hunt...not to catch a spider, but to watch her build her web – it is fascinating!

This is how she does it:

- She finds two supports – usually twigs or branches of trees.

- She connects a line between the two twigs by climbing from one to the other, unravelling her web as she goes along. But she may also let out a length of silk and wait for the wind to carry her across to the other branch or twig.

- She then drops another thread from the middle point of this line to anchor the web. The second thread forms a basic Y-shape, and gradually she adds more threads radiating out from the centre of the Y.
- Any insect that touches the web will set off a vibration and will be pounced on by the spider. Out of interest, weight-for-weight the spider's silk is stronger than steel cable.

Make a hairy, scary spider.

All you need is pipe-cleaners and a small magnet.

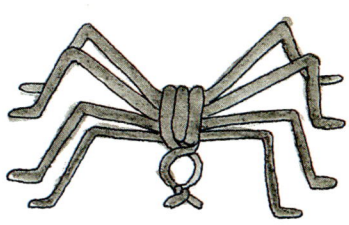

1. Lay four pipe-cleaners side by side. Measure their length and mark off the middle point.
2. Bend the fifth pipe-cleaner in half and, keeping the other four pipe-cleaners flat, wrap it around the centre of the four pipe-cleaners. Wrap the fifth pipe-cleaner around twice until both ends face forward – just as it is done in the drawing.

3. Twist the two open ends around twice and insert a pencil between them. Twist the two ends once again and then remove the pencil.

5. Bend the legs up from the body and then down again so that each leg has been bent in half. Then turn up the feet.
6. Spread the legs apart and adjust them to look like a real spider.

Leave your hairy, scary friend on Mum's pillow and wait for her squeal! If you have a small magnet, you could glue it to the underside of the spider's body and keep it on the fridge door.

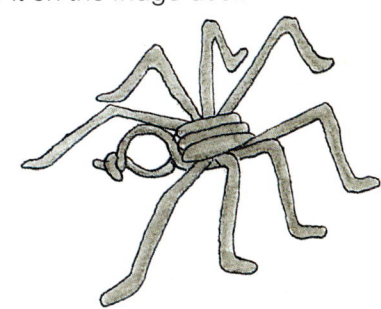

The Termite Mound

Scattered throughout the bush are strange-looking mounds of soil with peculiar shapes. Some are large and some fairly small. These are called termite mounds.

Did you know that these wonderful structures are built by tiny insects that are not larger than one of your toes?

That's right. The insects are called termites and the large mounds that they build so well are called termite mounds.

There are many different types of termites in the bush. One of them, the fungus grower, builds mounds that may even be taller than a man.

At home in a maze

Near the top of the mound there are a number of ventilation shafts which act as air pipes and extend down to the centre. These ventilation shafts can be opened and closed by the termites as the temperatures outside the mound changes, and in this way the temperature inside the mound is kept constant.

Just below the ground and near the centre of the mound is the central cavity where the termites live. This cavity may be a metre wide and is filled with little clay shelves which divide the cavity into a number of chambers.

Termite workers do most of the work in the mound.

Termite mounds may be twice as tall as a child.

The termites grow their fungus in some of the chambers near the top of the cavity. The fungus gardens are made from termite dung that is rolled up and shaped to make combs and shelves. They look like the inside of a walnut, are reddish brown in colour and are dotted with small white balls. These fungus balls are fed to the king and queen of the mound and also to the young termites.

In a termite mound nothing is wasted. When a termite eats, it digests and then regurgitates the food for another termite to eat, sometimes other termites even eat the termite's dung. In this way the food goes from one termite to the next until there is nothing left but a brown 'cement' which is then used to build the mound. Even termites that die in the mound are eaten and then go through this process.

Termite families

Living in the mound are a few different types of termites. The most common is the worker termite. It is small, colourless and blind and does all the work in the mound – building, feeding the king and queen and the soldiers, caring for the young and collecting food.

Soldier termites defend the nest from enemy attacks.

The workers feed and care for the queen termite.

The soldier termite only defends the mound against enemies. They have powerful pincers that they use to protect the other termites from attack. They are also blind and they cannot even feed themselves. The worker termites feed them.

Then, in a small chamber in the very centre of the mound are the king and queen termites. The queen can be 10 centimetres long and her abdomen is so swollen with eggs that her feet cannot touch the ground. Her main purpose is to produce eggs which are carried away by the workers to chambers where they hatch after about a month. These eggs develop into new workers and soldiers.

Send out the army
If you break open a termite mound, you will probably see the workers hard at work in the tunnels. But, as they realise that the mound has been disturbed, they rush back down into the depths of the mound and after a few minutes the soldier termites come up to the opening to defend the mound.

After the soldiers have seen off the danger, the workers return to the opening and begin to seal the holes with a regurgitated mixture of saliva and sand. Other workers go underground to collect grains of sand which they bring back up to the surface, covered in their saliva and deposit them around the openings. The saliva acts like cement and it hardens very quickly so that the mound becomes very difficult to break open.

The termites are active all day and they spend nearly their whole lives underground. They feed on dry grass, dead leaves, twigs, animal dung and dry wood. When they go to the surface to collect their food they build tunnels over themselves so that they are protected from the sun and enemies.

Enemies and destroyers
One of the termite's enemies is the antbear. It is a large anteater with a long nose and ears like a rabbit, and it has very powerful front claws which it uses to dig into termite mounds. Once it has broken a mound open the antbear pokes its long sticky tongue down the tunnels and the termites all stick to the tongue.

The antbear usually leaves a large hole in the termite mound and these holes are then used by many other animals as places of safety. Warthogs may change the mounds slightly and sleep in them during the night and porcupines and honey badgers will often sleep in them during the day. Hyaenas give birth to their cubs in large mounds and leopards also hide their cubs in these holes.

Old termite mounds are often used by other animals such as the mongoose.

The soil which is used to build the mound has been brought up from underground and is also covered with the termite's saliva, and it is very rich. Fruit-eating birds may perch on the termite mounds and often drop the seeds of fruit onto the mound. Before long trees and bushes spring up from these seeds and the mound eventually gets covered in vegetation.

The grasses and other plants growing on the mound are eaten by many animals and, because the mounds are so tall, they are ideal vantage points for predators. During a hunt, leopards and cheetahs will often climb onto a termite mound from which they can see the land around them and find their prey.

Raising a family

In spring, the queen termite lays eggs that eventually develop into termites with wings that are called nymphs. These winged termites are kept in the mound until the conditions outside are just right. After the rains, when the soil is wet and the temperatures are rising, the workers make little holes in the side of the mound and the soldiers come out and stand guard.

Lots of workers then come out of the holes and they are followed by the flying termites which immediately take off and fly away. After a few minutes, the workers close up the holes and wait for another day before letting even more flying termites free.

Leopards can see their prey from the tops of mounds.

The flying termites are very fat and are eaten by many different animals: frogs, lizards, scorpions, insects, spiders and birds. Few survive.

Those that survive eventually land on the ground and their wings fall off. Then they lift their tails and release a smell into the air that attracts the male flying termites.

When the male lands next to a female, he also loses his wings and together the termites walk off to look for a place to dig a hole and start a new mound. These two termites will become the king and queen of a new colony of termites.

Workers help the flying termites out of the mound.

Soldier termites guard the nymphs in the nest.

THINGS TO DO

The old fossils
Termites are fascinating. These liitle creatures which look very much like ants, are not ants at all. Scientists have found fossils of termite mounds dating back millions of years, and it is likely that termites have been on the earth for one hundred million years. This means that they have existed for longer than human beings have.

Find a way out
Find the starting point deep inside the termite mound and help the winged termites make their way to the exit so that they can start their maiden flight – and start a termite mound of their own.

Termites are social and live together in mounds. They can not survive on their own.

43

Animals of the Night

Visitors to game reserves may think that once the sun sets there are no animals to be seen. But there are many animals that wake up and are active only at night.

Animals that are most active at night are called *nocturnal* animals. Most nocturnal animals have vey good night vision which allows them to see in the darkness.

But why are some animals active in the day and some at night? One reason could be that this may reduce the amount of competition for food, with two different animals feeding on the same food, but at different times.

The king and the thief

It is possible to see lions in the daytime, but they are always sleeping. That's because lions are only really active at night. As soon as the sun sets, the lions get up, lick and clean one another, have a drink of water and then set off on the hunt.

If you look at a picture of a lion you can see that there are pale lines just under the lion's eyes. These marks help the lion to see better at night by reflecting more light into his eye.

The spotted hyaena is another nocturnal animal. It uses its very good sense of smell to find animals that have been killed by other animals such as the leopard. If the leopard doesn't hoist its kill into a tree, it will lose it to the hyaena. Although it gets most of its food in this way, the hyaena may also hunt for itself.

These are some of the larger animals that are quite well-known, but there are many other smaller animals that are also active at night.

Hyaenas scavenge for food at night.

Lines under the lion's eyes help it to see at night.

Jumping babies

If you shine a spotlight into the bush at night, you may notice bright red lights moving about among the trees. Sometimes the lights disappear and then reappear further away. Sometimes you can see the lights flying through the air from tree to tree. What could they be?

If you move closer you will see that those lights are the large round eyes of a tiny furry animal called a lesser bushbaby. Their large eyes help them to see where they are going at night.

If bushbabies were people, they would easily hold the world high-jump record. A little bushbaby that measures 35 centimetres from head to tail can easily jump a height of four metres. That is more than ten times its own height.

Bushbabies feed on insects and the gum from *Acacia* trees. As dawn breaks they go to sleep in hollow trees.

Scampering in the dark

On the ground, other animals scuttle around in the darkness too.

The civet looks like a spotted cat, but it is really a member of the mongoose family. It lives alone and feeds mainly on insects, fruit and small animals.

Civets always go back to the same place to leave their dung – these 'toilets' are called latrines.

The lesser bushbaby's big, round eyes shine brightly in the dark.

The white face of the barn owl reflects light into the owl's eyes so that it can see well in the dark.

The smell of these latrines indicates to other civets that the territory is occupied. You can always tell a civet's latrine because they are full of the whitened shells of millipedes, the civet's favourite food.

Another cat-like animal that is really one of the mongoose family is the large-spotted genet. It has very large ears which can detect the slightest rustle of an insect or mouse in the grass. Sometimes the genet hunts by sitting quietly on a branch with its ears moving from side to side. If something rustles nearby, it pounces.

The genet has an extremely long tail which it uses for balance as it climbs trees looking for roosting birds.

Ants for dinner

Have you ever stuck your head into an ant's nest? Probably not, because it would be really most unpleasant. Ants would crawl up your nose, bite your ears and get into your eyes. But there is an animal that can do this without any problems at all. This strange-looking animal is called a pangolin. It is also called the scaly anteater, because its body is completely covered in heavy, strong scales that protect it.

The pangolin has strong, hooked claws that it uses for digging open ant nests. It has no ears that stick out and it can open and close its nostrils. It also has very thick eyelids that protect its eyes against bites. When the pangolin sticks its head into the nest, it closes its eyes and nostrils. The ants crawl all over its face, but there is nothing for them to bite.

The genet's large ears hear even the faintest sounds.

Pangolins use their sharp claws to open ant nests.

Porcupines eat at night and sleep during the day.

Moths and many other insects are active at night.

Then the pangolin pokes its long sticky tongue down the ant tunnels. The ants stick to the tongue and the pangolin withdraws it and swallows all the ants.

Another strange-looking nocturnal animal is the porcupine. It is covered in long prickly quills which act as protection from predators. Porcupines eat bulbs, tubers and roots which they dig up with their front claws. They also feed on wild fruits, tree bark and even dead animals.

After their night of feeding, most porcupines disappear into old antbear holes in the termite mounds where they sleep for the day.

The big and the small

You probably all know what a hippo looks like, but have you ever seen one out of the water? Sometimes they come out and bask in the sun next to the river, but not many people have seen them away from the water.

Hippos stay in the water for most of the day and only come out at night to eat.

That is because hippos are nocturnal animals that get out of the water at night to eat their favourite food, which is grass. Sometimes they graze far from the river and, before the sun rises the next morning, they return to the water where they keep cool from the heat of the sun.

If you switch a light on in the bush at night, especially in summer, you will soon find hundreds of insects buzzing around it. Moths, antlions, mantids and many other insects are all active during the night.

These insects attract insect-eaters such as bats, which fly around in the darkness to catch flying insects such as moths.

Nightjars are nocturnal birds that make strange and beautiful calls at night. They also feed on insects which they catch as they fly.

So, before you go to sleep at night, think of all those little nocturnal animals that are just waking up as you close your eyes.

Nightjars swoop on insects that fly at night.

THINGS TO DO

Animals of the night
Below is a selection of animals commonly found in game reserves. Can you identify them all? Which ones are animals of the night?

Match the eyes
See if you can tell to which animals of the night these pairs of eyes belong.

Answers: a. pangolin b. rhino c. bat d. antbear e. hoopoe f. rat g. porcupine h. giraffe i. bushbaby

a-2, b-3, c-1.

How Animals Communicate

Did you know that although animals cannot talk, shout, laugh or sing, or even make hand-signals like you and your friends, they are able to communicate with each other?

Animals can *communicate* using *sound*. They use *signals* that other animals can see, just as we do.

In the summer, if you go into a quiet part of the garden or into a game reserve and sit quietly and listen, you will hear all kinds of *sounds* – birds calling, grasshoppers humming, crickets chirping, frogs croaking or lions roaring. All of these sounds communicate messages.

Messages of the bush

You have probably heard the many different noises that dogs often make. They growl if they're angry, whine if they're unhappy and bark if they're excited. Animals in the wild communicate in much the same way.

An *angry* lion will growl or snarl and hiss, and when a pride of lions moves through the bush at night they *maintain contact* with one another by means of soft low grunts.

A lion's teeth and jaws are extremely powerful.

Some animals do not allow animals of the same kind to come into their *territories* and they then communicate this by calls. Have you ever heard a lion roar or a hyaena whoop? These calls tell other lions and hyaenas that the areas are occupied.

Birds use their calls to proclaim territories as well as to *attract mates*. Birds in large colonies, such as gannets and penguins, have to find their mates amongst thousands of other birds. They do this by means of calls. Although the calls all sound much the same to us, the birds can tell one bird from another by their calls.

Sounding the alarm

Birds also have *alarm calls*. They make high-pitched sounds if danger such as a snake or owl threatens.

Other animals also have alarm calls. Impala give loud snorts when they see a predator such as a lion or a leopard and the kudu gives a loud bark for the same reason.

If you wanted to talk to somebody far away you would probably use the telephone. But what if there were no telephones? Some African tribal people communicate with one another over great distances by beating drums in different rhythms that have certain meanings.

King penguins live in large colonies and identify their mates by their calls.

The spotted-backed weaver is dull brown, but the males are bright yellow in the breeding season.

Most frogs croak loudly to attract mates during the mating season.

There are animals that communicate in this way too. The bearded woodpecker finds a large hollow tree and then rapidly taps its beak against it so that it makes a loud drumming sound. And the toktokkie beetle makes a drumming sound that other toktokkies can hear by tapping his body against the ground.

Some animals even make sounds that we cannot hear. Elephants make very deep rumbling sounds that other elephants can hear. In this way they communicate to one another without us knowing.

Body language

When you wave goodbye to somebody, or put your finger across your lips to tell somebody to be quiet, you are using a *signal* to communicate.

Animals also use signals to communicate. When you come home from school, your dog will jump up and down and wag his tail excitedly. He is signalling to you that he is happy.

In the wild, a lioness flicks her tail rapidly from side to side to warn you that she is *angry* and is about to charge. The position of an animal's body also communicates messages. If you see a lion in a crouching position slowly stalking forward, that immediately tells you that the lion is hunting. In this way, lions know what other lions are doing just from their body positions and how their tails move.

The colour parade

Birds also use a number of different signals to communicate. Weaver birds are dull brownish-coloured birds for most of the year, but in summer, when it is time to mate, the males develop a bright yellow plumage that tells female weavers that he is *looking for a mate*. There are many other birds that do this. Can you think of any?

When albatrosses find suitable partners, they signal to one another by spreading their wings and bobbing their heads up and down like two people dancing at a party. You probably all know what a peacock looks like with his beautiful tail fanned out to make a magnificent display.

The male agama lizard has a bright blue head that bobs up and down every time he sees another agama. He is telling other agamas that he is the dominant agama.

Some frogs and insects have *warning coloration* which tells predators that they are unpleasant to eat. The blister beetle often squirts a poisonous substance into the mouth of any animal that may attack it and birds that see the bright yellow and black beetle have learnt that the colours mean that the beetle will be distasteful.

The bright colours of the blister beetle warn predators that it tastes awful.

Leopards urinate on bushes to mark their territory.

Rhinos also mark their territory by squirting urine.

Smells that tell a story

Animals also use *smells* to communicate with one another. We have seen how lions and birds use sound to proclaim their territories, but there is another way that animals *proclaim territory* and that is by means of smells.

Leopards will often walk around their territories regularly squirting urine against bushes. They are leaving their smell behind to tell other leopards that the territory is occupied. If it is a female leopard that is doing the marking, then she could also be telling male leopards in the area that she is *looking for a mate*.

Rhinoceros bulls do the same thing. They scrape their feet on the ground and then squirt urine onto the ground.

They will also go to certain places in their own territory to leave their dung behind and will return again and again until there are large piles of dung. These are called *middens*, and they tell other bull rhinos that the territory is occupied.

Female rhinos and their young calves also visit these middens and when the male rhino returns he can smell if the female is ready for mating or not. These middens can be seen as 'centres of communication'.

Just as beetles use warning coloration to protect themselves, so some animals use smells to *warn predators*. Civets, genets and honey badgers give off awful smells if they have been attacked by predators. The result is that predators usually leave them alone.

Even flowers communicate

If you go into a garden in spring, you can smell the blossoming flowers. By means of these lovely smells, the flowers are communicating to insects that there is food available and the insects are attracted to the smells. Insects fly from flower to flower and help flowers to become pollinated.

Not all flowers smell lovely. Some flowers give off a strong stink that attracts certain bugs and flies. And many flowers only give off smells at night to attract nocturnal insects.

Next time you go to a game reserve, especially in summer, get your nose to do some work. Try to identify the many different smells and then see if you can find out what each smell is trying to communicate to other animals.

These are just some of the many different ways that animals communicate. Next time you go to a game reserve watch the animals closely. Listen to them too. See if you can work out how they are communicating with one another.

Bright flowers tell insects that food is available.

THINGS TO DO

Animal talk
You have learnt that all animals communicate, but they do not talk like we do. Do you know how these animals communicate with each other?

51

Big Cats

Of all the fascinating animals to be found in the game reserves, the most interesting are the big cats – lion, leopard and cheetah. But they are all as different as they look.

Each one of the big cats looks and behaves differently and because of this they are able to live together in the same areas.

We all know what a lion looks like. Lions are light brown and males have large furry manes. They have long tails with a black tuft on the end and their fur is short.

Leopards and cheetahs are both spotted, but their spots are different. The leopard's spots are arranged in little groups called rosettes and the cheetah's are just single black spots scattered over their bodies.

Telling the difference

There are other differences between leopards and cheetahs. The leopard is stockier, has thick strong legs with large front paws and a large head.

Male lions have manes which make them look bigger.

The cheetah is built to run at high speed. It has a small head, thin body and long thin legs with small feet. To make it lighter, it even has smaller teeth than leopards and lions.

All cats have claws they can draw back into their paws. This helps them to climb trees if they have to. But the cheetah is different. It cannot retract its claws at all. This is to help it run at high speeds. As it runs, its claws dig into the ground to give it more grip so that it can run faster.

These three big cats live in different types of vegetation. Leopards prefer very thick bush where they can hide when they stalk, while lions prefer woodland and cheetahs prefer open grasslands where it is easier for them to run after prey.

Leopards are always alone. The only time you are likely to see more than one leopard is when you see a mating pair or a female with her cubs. Because they are always alone, they have to hunt very carefully by using thick bush to hide in as they stalk as close as possible to their prey before they pounce.

The cheetah's thin body is built to run very fast.

Male cheetahs often live in groups of three or four.

Leopards hunt alone and hide in bushes or trees.

Lions are very social animals and are nearly always found in groups called prides. Sometimes there can be 30 or more lions in a pride. Lions in a pride hunt together and when they spot prey they spread out and surround it before one or two lions give chase. The more lions there are, the more success they have in killing something.

Female cheetahs live alone except when they are looking after cubs, while male cheetahs are often found in groups of three or four.

Lions sleep during the day and hunt at night.

The hunt is on

Cheetahs hunt by looking out for prey as they walk through the bush. When prey is spotted, they stalk slowly towards it and then start running. At top speed, the cheetah is the fastest animal on land, running at more than 70 kilometres an hour.

Leopards and lions use their large front paws to grab their prey. As they hold the prey down they bite into the neck and strangle the animal. Sometimes these powerful animals might even break the prey's neck.

Cheetahs' feet are too small to be effective for catching prey. But they have a small sharp claw just above the foot, called a dew claw, with which they strike the prey as they run. The claw hooks into the prey's skin and trips it up or pulls it down. Then the cheetah quickly grabs hold of the animal by biting it on the throat and strangling it.

Leopards hunt mostly at night but will also hunt during the day, even in the hottest part of the day.

Lions are very good at conserving energy and whenever they have a chance they sleep. Some lions sleep for more than 18 hours each day. When the sun sets, lions become active. They hunt right through the night, but they stop for many rests. As soon as the sun rises in the morning, they find a shady place to sleep.

Cheetahs are the weakest of the three cats and because of this they have to watch out for danger all the time. Lions, leopards and hyaenas will steal kills from cheetahs. The cheetah manages to survive by hunting during the day when these other predators are less active.

Leopard cubs are born in well-hidden lairs or caves.

Cheetahs cannot climb trees but they run very fast.

Leopards also have to be careful that they do not lose their kills to hyaenas and lions. They make sure that this does not happen by hoisting their kills into trees, well out of reach of other predators.

Cheetahs cannot do this, because they cannot climb trees. So when they make a kill, they settle down to feed immediately and try to eat as quickly as possible.

Because they are usually in groups and because they are so big and powerful, lions do not have to worry about losing their kills to other predators. They just feed lazily and often take rests in between feeds.

The young ones

Leopards give birth to their cubs in lairs such as gaps among rocks, holes in termite mounds or very dense patches of bush. They keep the cubs in these lairs for a few days at a time and then move them to new lairs. When the cubs are very small, the mother moves them by carrying them, but after a few weeks the cubs are able to follow the mother. Leopard cubs learn to climb trees at an early age, and if danger threatens they just scamper up the nearest tree.

When a lioness is ready to give birth, she leaves the pride and gives birth to her cubs in a dense patch of bush. If the other cubs in the pride are the same age as hers, she will take her cubs back to the pride when they are a few weeks old. But if the other cubs are older, she prefers to look after them on her own because there would be too much competition from the older cubs. Lion cubs are quite safe because they usually have the protection of the other lions in the pride.

But cheetah cubs are more vulnerable. They cannot climb trees to escape danger and the adult cheetah is too weak to provide much protection. All cheetah cubs can do is run from danger. But this is often not enough, so many cheetah cubs are killed before they grow up.

The biggest threat facing these wonderful big cats is Man. All over Africa people need more land on which to live. Areas where the big cats used to live are being cleared so that people can build houses and plant crops. This is very important for the people, but it is also important that we make sure that there are game reserves where the big cats can continue living together.

Lion cubs are guarded by other lions in the pride.

THINGS TO DO

Spot the cat
Here are the silhouettes of the three big cats we have been reading all about. Can you guess which cat is which? Which one does not have spots?

a.

b.

c.

See if you can identify the spots of each of the big cats and match them to the correct animal silhouette.

1

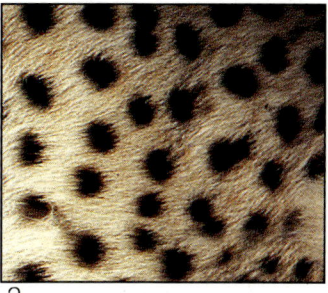
2

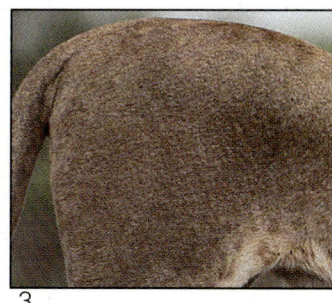
3

Answers: a. cheetah b. lion c. leopard; lions have no spots; a-2, b-3, c-1.

55

Elephants

It is the heaviest animal on land and the second tallest. It is grey, has large feet, big ears and a long trunk. You probably all know we are talking about an elephant.

Have you ever tried to lift up a car? It is almost impossible. The car is just too heavy. Did you know that an elephant can weigh as much as six cars? Imagine how heavy that must be. To stay as heavy as that, elephants have to eat a lot of food every day.

One long lunch

They spend all day and most of the night eating and at the end of each day they will have eaten food that weighs as much as three children.

Elephants eat fruit, leaves, grass, the bark of trees and other vegetation which they grind down with two sets of large teeth at the back of their mouths called molars.

As the elephant grows older, these molars wear down from the front of the mouth and new molars grow in from the back. At the end of the elephant's life, six sets of molars would have grown and been worn down.

Elephants use their trunks to drink from waterholes.

The world's biggest mammal

The most amazing thing about an elephant is its nose. It is called a trunk and looks like a long, fat hosepipe full of wrinkles. The elephant uses its trunk to sniff the air for danger, to smell all its favourite foods and to find other elephants. It is also used like a hand to pluck grass and leaves, break off branches, feel for objects and to suck up water for drinking.

There are two little 'fingers' at the end of an elephant's trunk which it uses for picking up small objects like berries.

Water is extremely important to elephants. They have to drink more than 150 litres each day and they use water to keep cool by spraying it over their bodies. When an elephant drinks, it sucks water up into its trunk and then squirts it into its mouth. Elephants have even been known to scare lions away by squirting water at them.

Did you know that elephants can go snorkelling? That's right. Elephants can walk across the very deepest rivers with their heads right under the water. Their trunks stick out above the surface just like a snorkel so that they can breathe.

Elephants eat about 300 kilograms of food in a day.

Elephant bulls fight one another for dominance.

Some elephants wallow in mud to protect their skin.

Look at the size of an elephant's ears. See how big they are? Elephants have very good hearing, but there is yet another reason for having such large ears.

They use their ears to help them keep cool, which can be very difficult for such a large animal. All the blood in the elephant's body flows through a network of vessels in the ears. When it is very hot, the elephant flaps his ears and this cools the blood which flows back into the body at a lower temperature.

At home in the wild

Elephants can be colourful. All over Africa, there are many elephants of different colours – red, brown, black, grey and even white. This is because elephants love to wallow in mud. They throw mud and sand over their bodies to protect themselves from the many biting insects that land on their skin.

In some parts of Africa the soil is mostly red, in other parts the soil is almost white. After the elephant has been to the mud to wallow, it takes on the colour of the soil in that area. But if you wash all the soil off an elephant, you'll find that its skin is actually a grey colour.

Elephants have large round feet that look like cushions. This allows them to walk very silently through the bush, but it also softens their footfall so that they do not damage their legs as they walk carrying all that weight.

Elephants make many different sounds. If an elephant is angry or upset, it will trumpet loudly, squeal or scream. The sound of an angry elephant is very frightening.

The elephant's padded feet allow it to walk quietly.

Elephants communicate with each other by making low rumbling sounds like stomach rumbles and other sounds we cannot hear.

Most elephants live in small family groups made up mostly of female elephants with their sisters and cousins, and their young calves. Sometimes different family groups come together to form large herds called breeding herds.

Most male elephants live in separate groups and they will only join the breeding groups when the females are ready for mating.

Elephants do not need much sleep, and sleep for only about one hour each day. When an elephant wants to sleep, it searches for a large termite mound and lies down against it. In places where there are no termite mounds, such as in the desert, elephants sleep against large bushes.

Male elephants are called elephant bulls.

Elephants are social animals and live in herds.

The elephant bull's white tusks are made of ivory and some people kill elephants to sell the ivory.

An elephant's treasure

Elephants have long, sharp, white tusks made of ivory. They use their tusks to defend themselves against danger, to dig for water, to break branches and to strip bark off trees.

Just like us, some elephants can be left-handed or right-handed. The tusk they prefer to use is called the master tusk and you can tell which one it is because it is usually worn down more than the other tusk.

Some elephants have tusks that are so long that they nearly touch the ground.

But these tusks can cause problems. Man has found that the ivory can be very useful for making beautiful carvings and jewellery. Some people will pay a lot of money for ivory.

Many poor people with no money will go out into elephant areas and illegally shoot them to take their tusks. Unfortunately, many elephants are killed in this way and they are now getting less and less. If something isn't done to stop this killing, then one day there may be no elephants.

In places where elephant populations are decreasing, game rangers have to stop the people who are killing the elephants. But in other areas, where elephants are protected, they are increasing in numbers and are starting to damage the enviroment by knocking down too many trees. Game rangers then have to shoot some of the elephants to stop the damage. The rangers then sell the tusks and they use the money to improve conditions for the animals in the reserves.

So, you see it is not so easy to solve the problem. In some places we have to stop the killing altogether, and in other places the tusks can help to save our wildlife.

THINGS TO DO

Making your own elephant
With just a few toilet roll tubes and a stapler you can make your own elephant.

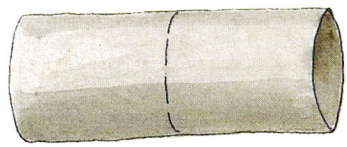

1. Cut one tube in half – now you have two which will be the elephant's legs.

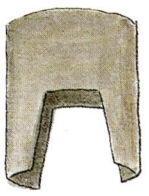 

2. Cut two triangles out of each half of the tube and staple the two halves together as it is shown in the drawing above.

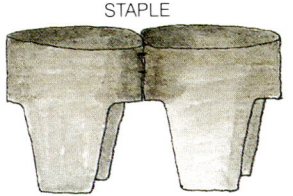

STAPLE

3. Take another tube and cut out the trunk and the tusks as shown in the drawing. But don't throw away the pieces you have cut away – these will be the elephant's big ears, while the other piece will be the elephant's head.

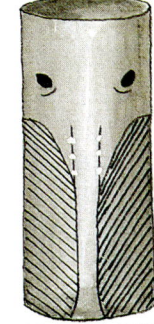

SLASH ALONG DOTTED LINE

THE SHADED SECTION IS USED FOR THE ELEPHANTS EARS

4. Roll the trunk around a pencil so that it will curl, and staple the elephant's ears to its head.

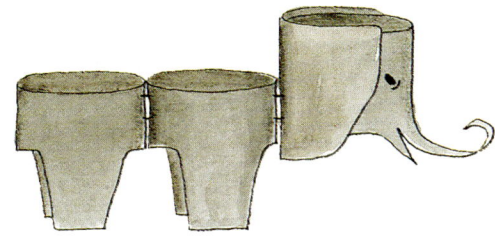

5. Then staple the head to the front pair of legs.

FOLD SLASH TAIL END

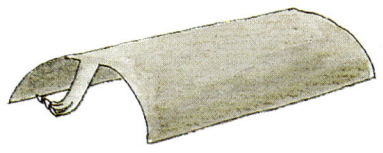

6. To make the elephant's back, take the third tube and cut straight down its length. Then flatten it slightly and cut out the tail as it is shown in the drawing.
7. Staple the sides of the body onto the legs, making sure that the tail is in the centre.
Now that you know how to make one elephant, you can make a whole herd!

Caring for the Earth

Have you ever wondered how we all manage to stay alive? Without us realizing, there are many things happening on this earth that make sure we all stay alive.

The huge forests growing in South America and other parts of the world provide us all with oxygen so that we can breathe.

Some of the sun's rays can actually be harmful to us and can cause cancer, but there is a layer of the earth's atmosphere, called the ozone layer, that protects us from harmful rays.

The earth's atmosphere acts like a blanket and keeps us from getting too hot or too cold. And the rivers and lakes provide us all with pure drinking water we need in order to stay alive.

Don't kill the world

But these wonderful and extremely important resources are all being destroyed by Man. The forests are being cut down so that we can use the land for farming and so that the wood can then be turned into paper and furniture.

The clean air is being polluted by factories and cars that pump gases and other poisons into the atmosphere. These gases are also heating up the atmosphere, so if we do not do something soon, the earth will become too hot.

Beautiful forests are being cut down to make paper.

Factories and farmers are pouring poisonous chemicals into the rivers and lakes so that we cannot drink the water any more.

The ozone layer is slowly being destroyed by chemicals called CFCs which are produced by aerosols, fridges and plastics.

We are producing so much rubbish that there is hardly any space left for us to bury it all. Paper, plastic, glass, cardboard and even tin cans lie scattered all around us, making the countryside ugly and often harming the animals that live in those areas.

These are very, very big problems and you probably think that they are too big for you to handle. But there are many things you can do to help care for the earth.

Save our forests

Let us start by saving the forests. You can help to replace the trees that are being cut down by planting trees in your garden at home, or in your school grounds. Tell your friends to do the same and ask them to pass on the message. Think of the forests we could make if we all planted just one tree.

The rubbish we throw away can destroy our environment.

The glass bottles thrown into bins such as these are recycled and made into new bottles.

The plastic from which these styrofoam boxes are made produce chemicals which harm the ozone layer.

Did you know that paper is made from trees? Every time you throw a piece of paper into the rubbish bin, you are throwing away part of a tree. But paper can be recycled. There are places that collect old paper and turn it into new paper.

Instead of just throwing all your paper into the rubbish bin, collect it and, when you have a good supply, take it to a recycling centre. Your old paper will then be turned into new paper and you may well have saved quite a few trees from being chopped down.

Recycling old for new

There are other things you can recycle. Tin cans are made from metal called aluminium which is very important for building aeroplanes, cars and other important things. There is a limited amount of aluminium in the earth and if we are not careful with it, it will all be used up soon.

If you collect the tin cans and take them to a recycling centre, you would then be helping to conserve aluminium *and* you would also be reducing the amount of rubbish lying around.

Glass can be recycled too. But you have to separate the different coloured glass bottles into different containers before you take them to be recycled into new bottles.

And what about the hole in the ozone layer? Today people can make aerosols, fridges and plastics without CFCs which are the chemicals that break down the ozone. Next time your family goes shopping, make sure that they buy aerosols that are marked 'ozone-friendly'.

Styrofoam is a plastic that produces CFCs and it can never be broken down. That means that a piece of styrofoam that is thrown onto the ground today will still be exactly the same if somebody found it a thousand years from now.

Many fast-food restaurants pack their food into styrofoam containers. Ask these restaurants to supply your food in cardboard packs and explain to them why. If they refuse, then buy your food at a restaurant that does.

Aerosol cans which do not damage the ozone layer often carry an 'ozone friendly' label.

A breath of fresh air

How can you help control the air pollution that is causing the atmosphere to heat up? Well, you can start by walking or riding your bicycle instead of going by car every time. You can also ask your parents to form lift clubs with your friends' parents so that you can all travel in one car. In this way, cars are used less often and less fumes are pumped into the air.

Many of the fumes and gases polluting our air come from power stations that supply us with electricity. The more electricity we use, the more gases the power stations produce. We can help reduce these gases by saving on the amount of electricity we use.

There are many ways we can do this. If you do not need a light on in the house, switch it off. If you're not watching television, turn the set off and if you go away on holiday ask your parents to switch off the geyser.

Save water

All our drinking water comes from rivers, lakes and dams and the amount of water always stays the same. But there are more and more people every year who drink this water. So it is very important that we look after it.

We can save water in many different ways. For example, you can use less water in the toilet by putting a brick or a large two-litre bottle filled with sand into the cistern. Less water will be used every time the toilet is flushed.

Plastic and other chemicals can pollute our water.

And leaking taps cause a large amount of water to be wasted every year. Check all the taps in your house for leaks and ask an adult to have it fixed.

You may be able to think of many other ways to save water and electricity, and prevent littering.

We must remember that, just like the oxpecker and the buffalo, we must develop a mutualistic relationship with the earth, if we want to survive. These are some of the things we can do.

Power stations and factories produce smoke and gases which pollute the air.

If we do not take care of the world we live in our environment may soon look like this.

THINGS TO DO

Making your own paper

Have you ever thought of recycling old newspapers? Making your own paper is really quite easy! All you need is some newspaper, a wooden board, some cloth, a bucket, a plastic bowl, a plastic bag, a wooden spoon and some wire mesh (about 30 cm x 30 cm) which you can buy from any hardware store.

1. Soak the newspaper in water. Drain off the water and then, using the wooden spoon, mash the paper so that it looks almost like porridge.

2. Put the mashed newspaper into the plastic bowl and then add as much water as there is pulp, carefully mixing the two together. If you want to make coloured paper, you could add some powdered paint!
3. Place the piece of wire mesh into the bowl so that when you take it out, the mesh is covered with the mashed newspaper.

4. Lay the cloth on the wooden board and then put the mesh face down on the cloth. When you lift the wire off the paper pulp, make sure that the pulp stays behind on the cloth.

5. Once you have removed the wire, firmly press the extra water out of the pulp using some cloth.

6. When you have pressed out all the water you can, put a clean sheet of plastic over the pulp and then place some heavy objects (thick books are just right!) onto the plastic.
7. Leave everything as it is for a whole day. When the pulp is really dry, remove the books and the plastic...and you have recycled colour paper.

Making your own toys

Have you noticed how many interesting bits and pieces are thrown in the rubbish bin at home? There are egg cartons, boxes, cardboard tubes, scraps of cloth, match boxes, bottle tops, pieces of paper, string and plastic. You could collect all these things and make your own toys: cars and aeroplanes; a zoo of animals such as a lion, a baboon, and a peacock; all sorts of interesting hats; a doll's house and even some furniture. See how many different toys you can make!

Index

aerial roots 20, 22
aerosol 60
agama lizard 49
air pollution 60, 62
alarm calls 12, 48
albatross 29, 30, 49
antbear 22, 41
antelope 13, 14, 33
antlion 9, 46
ants 45
arachnids 36
armour-plating 13
atmosphere 60-62
baboon 6, 8
baboon spider 38
balance 6
bark spider 12, 37
barn owl 25, 26
barred owl 26
bats 46
beaks 21, 24, 28, 49
birds 9, 12, 16, 18, 20, 24, 28-30, 33, 42, 49
birds of prey 24, 30
birth 4, 8, 54
black button spider 38
blister beetle 49
bones 28
brakes 6, 30
browsers 16
buffalo 16, 20
Burchell's starling 22
bushbaby 44
bushbuck 5
butterfly 9, 12
camouflage 12
carnivores 17
caterpillar 9, 14
cattle egret 22
CFCs 60, 61
chameleon 6
cheetah 6, 10, 17, 42, 52-55
chemical defences 13
chicks 9, 26
civet 44, 45, 50
claws 14, 21, 45, 46, 52, 53
climbing mouse 6
cobra 14
colonies 48
coloration 12, 26, 49, 50, 57
commensalism 21
communication 4-6, 48-51, 57
competition 16, 44
conservation 58, 60-63
contact 4, 5, 48
creeping scorpion 37
crocodile 6, 17, 33
cycles 16-18

defences 12-15
dikkop 9
disease 20, 21
dog 5, 33, 48, 49
duiker 16
dung 17, 18, 44
eagle 24, 30
ears 25, 29, 32, 45, 57
eggs 8, 9, 10, 18, 41, 42
electricity 62
elephant 4, 10, 14, 16, 18, 32, 49, 56-58
Emperor moth 12
escape 12, 30
eyes 12, 24, 44, 46
factories 60
falcon 24
feathers 6, 25, 28-30, 49
feeding 16-18
feet 57
fish 6, 10, 17, 18
flight 25, 28-30, 34
flowers 50
fly-swats 6
flycatchers 22
following signals 4, 5
forests 60
forktailed drongo 22
frog 9, 10, 13, 18
fungus grower 40-41
gannet 48
gemsbok 33
genet 6, 45, 50
gestation 10
giant eagle owl 22
giraffe 8, 14, 16, 17, 20, 22
glass 61
golden orb-web spider 37
goshawk 18
grasshopper 13
grazers 16
ground beetle 13
hare 8
hawk 24, 30
hearing 12, 25, 57
heart 28
herbivores 16
herds 14, 57
hippopotamus 13, 14, 32, 46
honey badger 50
honeybee 21
honeyguide 21
hornbill 18
horns 14
host 20, 22
hunting 5, 10, 24, 26, 38, 42, 44, 45, 52, 53
hunting spider 38

hyaena 8, 17, 41, 44, 48, 53-54
impala 8, 10, 12, 14, 22, 33, 48
insectivores 18
insects 10, 12, 18, 22, 37
ivory 58
jackal 13
Kalahari Desert 33, 34
kudu 5, 12, 16, 33
lair 8, 54
larvae 9
leopard 6, 8, 13, 17, , 33, 41, 42, 50, 52-55
lion 4, 5, 8, 10, , 17, 33, 44, 48, 49, 52-55
lizard 18
longtailed widow 6
lungs 28
maggots 17
mammals 8, 28, 29
manes 52
mantid 46
marsh owl 24
marsh harrier 24
mating 6, 48, 49, 50
metal 61
midden 50
millipede 13, 45
mistletoe 20
molars 56
mongoose 13
monitor lizard 6
monkey 6, 8
mortality 10
moth 9, 46
mud 32, 57
muscles 28, 29
mutualism 20
nests 9, 21, 22, 38, 45
night 33, 37, 38, 44-47
nightjar 12, 18, 46
nocturnal 44-47, 50
nyala 5
nymphs 42
ostrich 9
otter 6
owls 24-26
oxpecker 20, 21
ozone layer 60, 61
ozone-friendly
pangolin 6, 13, 45, 46
paper 60-62
paradise whydah 6
parasites 20
parasitism 20
peacock 49
penguin 48
pincers 36, 37, 41
plants 16, 17, 18, 42, 50
plastic 60-61
plover 9
poison 26, 36, 38, 49, 60
pollination 50
pollution 60-62
porcupine 14, 22, 46
power stations 62
predators 4, 6, 8, 10, 12, 13, 14, 17, 18, 22, 42, 48, 50, 54
prides 53, 54
protection 6, 13, 32, 41, 54, 57
queen termite 40-42
quills 14
rabbit 8
recycling 61-62

relationships 20-22
reptiles 9, 28
resources 60
resting 33, 44, 53, 57
rhinoceros 5, 16, 22, 32, 50
rock scorpion 37
rosettes 52
scales 13, 45
scavengers 17
scops owl 18, 26
scorpions 36-38
senses 12
signals 4, 5, 48, 49
skeletons 28
smell 12, 50, 56
snail 13
snakes 18
social spider 38
soil 16
soldier termite 40-42
sounds 26, 48, 49, 57
sparrowhawk 18
spiders 18, 36-38
spots 52
squirrel 5, 12, 16, 18
stick insect 12
stings 14, 36
stink bug 13
stork 30
strangler fig 20
streamlining 29
styrofoam 61
sun 16, 22, 32, 60
swallow 18, 22
swift 22
tadpoles 9
tails 4-7, 21, 36, 37, 45, 49, 52
talons 24
temperature 32-34, 46, 57, 60
termite mound 8, 13, 22, 40-43, 54, 57
termites 16, 17, 18, 22, 34, 40-43
terrapin 13
territories 26, 48, 50
thermals 30
tick 20, 21, 36
torchwood tree 18
tortoise 13
tree orchid 22
trunk 56
tusks 14, 58
urine 50
venom 14, 37
ventilation 34, 40
vulture 17, 30
Wahlberg's eagle 22
warblers 18
warthog 5, 10, 14, 16, 22, 32
waterbuck 4, 33
waterholes 32, 33
weaver bird 34, 49
webs 28, 37
weight 56, 57
wild dog 5, 10
wildebeest 8, 10, 14, 16
wings 12, 25, 28-30, 49
wolf spider 38
woodborer beetle 18
woodpecker 18, 49
worker termite 40-42
young 8-10, 54
zebra 6, 8, 14, 16